PARMENIDES

AND

THE WAY OF TRUTH

PARMENIDES

AND

THE WAY OF TRUTH

Translation and Commentary by

Richard G. Geldard

Monkfish Book Publishing Company
Rhinebeck, New York

Monkfish Book Publishing Company
27 Lamoree Road
Rhinebeck, N.Y. 12572

Printed in The United States of America.
Book and cover design by Georgia Dent.
Cover art by Astrid Fitzgerald
No. 278 - Encaustic, Litho Crayon and Collage on Wood, 12"H x
12"W x 1"D, 2006

Library of Congress Cataloging-in-Publication Data

Geldard, Richard G., 1935-
  Parmenides and The way of truth : translation and commentary / by
Richard G. Geldard.
     p. cm.
  Includes bibliographical references.
  ISBN 978-0-9766843-4-3
  1. Parmenides. I. Title.
B235.P24G47 2007
182'.3--dc22

                              2007029818

              10 9 8 7 6 5 4 3 2 1

Bulk purchase discounts for educational or promotional purposes are
available.
              Monkfish Book Publishing Company
                      27 Lamoree Road
                  Rhinebeck, New York 12572
                  www.monkfishpublishing.com

To Astrid, Always

TABLE OF CONTENTS

Introduction... vii

Chapter 1 – Parmenides of Elea........................... 1

Chapter 2 – The Fragments................................. 20

Chapter 3 – Wrestling With Parmenides............. 52

Chapter 4 – The Way of Truth............................. 92

Chapter 5 – From Being to Consciousness......... 109

Glossary... 127

Suggested Reading... 128

Endnotes.. 129

INTRODUCTION

TWENTY-FIVE CENTURIES AGO, at a point in history the Greeks called the 69th Olympiad and we moderns now label 500 BCE, the known world from the Mediterranean basin east into India and China experienced a Great Awakening. The ancient mythological world view, in which a pantheon of disparate gods ruled human imagination, was under siege, and new teachers emerged to address new questions about the meaning of human existence and destiny.

Called The Axial Age by Karl Jaspers, The Great Leap of Being by Eric Voegelin and others, and The Age of Transformation by Karen Armstrong, the era in question actually encompassed four or five hundred years, beginning around 800 BCE and ending around 200 BCE. But for the purposes of this study, the years close to 500 BCE were pivotal. Figures such as the Buddha, Confucius, Pythagoras, Heraclitus, and Parmenides, to name a few of the master teachers, were revealing a new understanding of the human condition and its relationship to society, nature and divinity.

It was the time of the birth of philosophy, beginning with a new understanding of natural science, which in turn led to rational exploration of the mysteries of the cosmos. Emerging as well was a new sense of personal human freedom and the resulting concerns for morality and ethics. Societies had to create new laws dealing with social order and justice. Among the Greeks, these early thinkers and law makers were called *aletheia*, those who uncover the truth, or truth-sayers. Later, as a political and practical matter, they became *philosophoi*, lovers of wisdom.

One such philosopher was the Ionian Heraclitus, who said, *"It is wise to agree that all things are One."*[1] This startling and challenging definition of reality was one of the seminal ideas of the Great Leap of Being. It may have been wise, but it is also profoundly difficult to grasp, which is where his contemporary Parmenides enters the picture. What we have of his poem "On Nature" explores the truth of reality in the light of ideas of unity. In that respect he is similar to Heraclitus, but their methods were very different. Parmenides revealed for the first time a vision of Being not confounded with human attributes. He invented ontology, the philosophy of Being. And at the same time, he revealed a world seen through Being, as opposed to a world seen through ordinary human thought, or opinion, and philosophy has been wrestling with these same questions (and opinions) ever since.

Parmenides of Elea is preeminent among the members of the Eleatic School, philosophers who lived and worked on the western coast of Italy, in what in the sixth century BCE was a small Greek colony. Usually, the Eleatics include Xenophanes, Parmenides, and Zeno. Because of their fragmentary history, their uncertain biographies, their style of exploration, the Eleatics present a special challenge but also a special opportunity. The challenge is clear enough. How can we draw coherent conclusions about their thought from fragmentary remains? How can we know what is missing from the record?

Consider the case of Ludwig Wittgenstein in this regard. What would have happened had his later works, such as the tantalizing

On Certainty, been lost and all we had was the early *Tracticus?* It is possible, but doubtful, that commentators would have teased out the later views from between the lines of Wittgensteins's core work and comments about him from later thinkers, who had read *On Certainty*.

For example, the last entry (#676) in *On Certainty* questions the state of reality. "I cannot seriously suppose that I am at this moment [writing this] dreaming. Someone who, dreaming, says 'I am dreaming,' even if he speaks audibly in doing so, is no more right than if he said in his dream, 'it is raining,' while it was in fact raining. Even if his dream were actually connected with the noise of the rain."

In another telling passage (#532) Wittgenstein wrote, "So when [G.E.] Moore sat in front of a tree and said, 'I know that that's a tree,' he was simply stating the truth about his state at the time." We can't be sure, Wittgenstein implies, about the tree at all. We are interested in that "state" in philosophy. Are we in some sense dreaming when we are awake? What is this so-called "reality" we see, hear, taste, touch and smell? What is its nature? What are its laws? When philosophers speak of "awakening" to the real nature of things, what do they really mean? An altered state? Do they imply that there is a "state" in which an individual may come to differentiate between the truth of reality and the perceptions of sensory information? Some would say, "Of course." Others would say that what our senses tell us (and by that we mean all the instruments our brains have devised) is what is. Anything else is beyond our grasp. Is it? What can I know? philosophy asks, and how best do I pursue this knowledge?

The task of looking again at the fragments of the Presocratics offers, I believe, a way into this dilemma. The opportunities which arise from writing analytically about such fragmentary work are intriguing. The commentator is forced to build bridges across wide chasms of doubtful data. Interpretations must be offered as speculative. The murky depths of intuitive speculation have to be exposed to review by other intuitive thinkers or condemned by rationalists as wild and philosophically unsound. But the results, even if doubtful to some, may be valuable in the long run because a certain purity resides in the effort. Those who begin the task have the privilege of clarity, even when later seekers have only fragmentary evidence of those beginnings.

In the case of Parmenides in particular the challenge is great because some of the fragments of his poetic treatise have been seized upon as the beginning of the scientific method, thus placing him in the equation-dominated world of modern speculation. On the other hand, others have seized upon his more metaphysical statements as evidence of a mystical or shamanistic turn of mind, uniting him with Pythagoras and placing him outside the exoteric tradition. Thus, he is a friend of several disparate traditions.

The purpose of returning to reassess Parmenides and the Presocratics in this case is literally to begin again, to learn from centuries of dead ends and blunted attempts just how and why the philosophic enterprise has argued itself into paralysis and gnostic dissatisfaction. It is as if today philosophy sits quietly in a wheelchair in a nursing home run by science, looking out at the scudding clouds, with its memories of great achievements. Meanwhile, out on the lawn and in the basement laboratories, the physicists and biologists appear in ruddy health, enjoying the dance of particles and the advances in technology. For the moment, at any rate, they are firmly in charge.

What I propose here is to view the fragments of Parmenides as an exploration into the nature of unity and to see if Heraclitus was right when he said that it is wise to agree that all things are One. Or as Rumi wrote:

> When you see the splendor of union,
> the attractions of duality seem poignant
> and lovely, but much less interesting.

Chapter 1 – Parmenides of Elea

T HE BIOGRAPHY OF Parmenides really begins several
generations before his birth. In the mid-sixth century
BCE, in the Greek city-state of Phokia, in Ionia (now
modern Turkey), just east of the island of Chios, the Phokians
were on the verge of losing their tenuous purchase on the Asian
land mass. Daily life for these Greek sailors and traders was a balance of fierce tradition and delicate accommodation. The Lydian
and Phrygian influences in matters of religion and culture were
constant intrusions in all the coastal colonies in Asia Minor. As
a result, life in Phokia was an exercise in constant adjustment,
defending traditions of language and belief while absorbing new
influences. It was the price of living on the eastern fringes of Hellenic culture.

The most important influences, aside from economic and
military ones, were religious. The Phokians, like most Ionians,
generally followed Homer and Hesiod in matters of the gods,
and Delphi was the navel of their universe, but from the hills
of Phrygia (Anatolia to us now), the influence of the ancient
Mother Goddess flowed west from the mountain streams down
into the valleys and coastal ranges. The great sanctuary of Artemis at Ephesus, some sixty miles to the south of Phokia, was
the Hellenic center of the Earth Mother cults, and Cybele, an-

cient Titanic mother of the gods, was alive and well in the nearby mountains.

In 545 BCE, under the leadership of Cyrus, the emerging Persian empire swept to the northwest from their strongholds in Persepolis and Babylon, conquered Asia Minor and drove the Phokians from their lands. Most of the survivors sailed south to settle Cyprus, but a few sailed west, past Athens and the Peloponnese, and passing through the treacherous straits of Messina and the famed Scylla rock, sailed north to settle Hyele (Elea). Here, in gratitude for their survival, they erected a temple to Poseidon, god of the sea, and an Ionic temple to a goddess not known to us, but possibly either Artemis, Demeter, or a goddess reflective of the Earth Mother.

The acropolis of the new town, sitting on a ridge of land and cutting the sloping fertile valley in half, looked out to sea and each day, the Phokians could watch the sun fall below the horizon, just as they did in their old home. But of course, it was not the same. The Phokians, now Hyeleans, suffered the pangs of intense loss; families torn apart, community sundered, and culture fragmented. All this had to be replaced, built anew. The first step was to find in the landscape and the heavens those familiar patterns which symbolized attachment to their divinities. The river flowing west down to the shore from the mountains to the east was the same as in the past. The gullies and ridges proclaimed the presence of the Earth Mother in her nurturing capacities of fecundity and sanctuary. The newly constructed acropolis, with its protective walls and temple, warned the active pirates on the islands to the south that here were people prepared to defend their new home. And the stability of the heavens above them must have been reassuring, too. Where Phokia was below the

40th parallel, Elea was just above, but the constellations in the night sky were the same.

What the new Hyeleans also had was structure and an effective political hierarchy. The prominent families took control and devised laws to govern the new enterprise. In the years to come, a mature Parmenides would be called upon to revise these laws and in the process earn the respect of his townspeople. But in the meantime Hyele thrived and even earned a reputation for religious and intellectual tolerance. Xenophanes, the peripatetic poet and professional wanderer, who was exiled from Colophon for insulting the gods, finally settled in Hyele and found it to his liking.

It was here, then, in 515 BCE (or the 65th Olympiad) that Parmenides was born, the son of Pyres, heir to a family of high rank. He received the best education, which included training in geometry and philosophy from a poor, displaced Pythagorean named Ameinias. Years later, Parmenides erected a monument to Ameinias to honor his former teacher. He did not erect one to Xenophanes the Cynic. It is unfortunate, in fact, that most biographers describe Parmenides as a student and follower of Xenophanes. He may have been the former, but certainly not the latter.

As is the case with most of the Presocratics, we know very little of the early life of Parmenides. We are told only that he studied philosophy, that he devised the laws of his polis and that the citizens regarded the town's wealth and prosperity a direct result of those laws. He lived an exemplary life – what later became known among the Greeks as a "Parmenidean Life" and that he lived many years.

Early Influences

The presence of Xenophanes in Hyele (Elea) was certainly a pervasive influence on the future philosopher. If we take 500 BCE as a starting point in the intellectual education of Parmenides, about fifteen at the time, he would have been introduced to the essential views of the aging Xenophanes. The extant fragments tell a mixed story.

First are the more famous – or notorious – fragments from Xenophanes dealing with the nature of the gods.

The numbering is Freeman's:[2]

11. *Both Homer and Hesiod have attributed to the gods all things that are shameful and a reproach among mankind: theft, adultery, and mutual deception.*

14. *But mortals believe the gods to be created by birth, and to have their own (mortals') raiment, voice and body.*

15. *But if oxen (and horses) and lions had hands or could draw with hands and create works of art like those made by men, horses would draw pictures of gods like horses, and oxen of gods like oxen, and they would make the bodies (of their gods) in accordance with the form that each species itself possesses.*

This curt dismissal of the Olympian system must have sent Xenophanes packing from his home in Colophon, that and his criticism of how the men of Colophon had assumed opulent Lydian ways. Not even Socrates nor the irascible Heraclitus were as pointed in their dismissal of the myth-o-poetic hierarchy. We see this argument today when intellectuals dismiss the notion of a personal god, a father-figure who answers prayers and cares for his children in favor of an indifferent universe. Most people in the ancient world were no different from those in our own who believe in the God described in the Bible as the deity who made human beings in His own image.

The problem for Xenophanes was no doubt his sarcasm in expressing his views. Other good minds were just as critical of tales of human depravity among the immortals. The real issue had to do with the very nature of God, of what it meant to be immortal. More heresy was to follow, but in this case, less insulting and more reflective, for example:

23. *There is one god, among gods and men the greatest, not at all like mortals in body or in mind.*

24. *He sees as a whole, thinks as a whole, and hears as a whole.*

25. *But without toil he sets everything in motion, by the thought of his mind.*

26. *And he always remains in the same place, not moving at all, nor is it fitting for him to change his position at different times.*

Although these fragments remove some of the anthropomorphic attributes of the deity, some remain. This god is male, possesses senses, actively sets things in motion, and remains in one place. Thus, Xenophanes made a series of choices, based on what, exactly, we have no clear idea. Parmenides must have asked, "Why this and not that? What, Xenophanes, lies behind your particular portrait?"

Another aspect of the presence of Xenophanes would have been more important to Parmenides than early speculations on the nature of God or gods. The old peripatetic poet often performed his own work at symposia, and the young Parmenides would probably have been present. In one important elegy, Xenophanes celebrated the ideal symposium, that gathering of men on couches, to eat, drink wine, tell stories and discuss the issues of the day. From earliest times, back into the heroic past when kings and heroes gathered around the hearth in the palace megaron, the symposium had been the central event of community. We learn from Plato and the example of Alkibiades just how easy it was to disrupt the proper ambiance of such a dinner with drunken behavior and excess.

In the ideal symposium, after the meal was over, the fish bones and other waste were cleaned from the tiled floor, the mixing bowls for wine and water were brought in, and musicians entered the room to entertain. As the evening grew late, and if the company was sober enough, discussions took place, some on philosophic subjects, including, no doubt, the nature of the gods. What follows from Xenophanes is one of finest descriptions we have of an ideal symposium:

> For now, behold, the floor is clean, and so too the hands of all, and the cups. One (attendant) places woven garlands round our heads, another proffers sweet-scented myrrh in a saucer. The mixing-bowl stands there full of good cheer, and another wine is ready in the jar, a wine that promises never to betray us, honeyed, smelling of flowers. In our midst the frankincense gives forth its sacred perfume; and there is cold water, sweet and pure. Golden loaves lie to hand, and the lordly table is laden with cheese and with honey. The altar in the center is decked with flowers all over, and song and revelry fill the mansion.
>
> It is proper for men who are enjoying themselves first of all to praise God with decent stories and pure words. But when they have poured a libation and prayed for the power to do what is just – for thus to pray is our foremost need – it is no outrage to drink as much as will enable you to reach home without a guide, unless you are very old. But the man whom one must praise is he who after drinking expresses thoughts that are noble, as well as his memory

concerning virtue allows, not treating of the battles of the Titans or of the Giants, figments of our predecessors, nor of violent civil war, in which tales there is nothing useful; but always to have respect for the gods, that is good.

The importance of this poetic celebration of the ideal symposium is not only its picture of proper decorum, but also its god-centered hierarchy. The central altar and the sense that telling appropriate stories in effect praising God sets a tone emulated by Plato's symposium, a feast which Alkibiades nearly ruins with his drunken intrusion. In this case it takes Socrates to bring order back to the proceedings. These descriptions are symbolic representations of the structure of Greek society and the role of religious order. They are also an apt description of what may be meant as "the Parmenidean Life."

Another aspect of the education of the young philosopher is touched upon in a satiric poem by Xenophanes in which he complains that athletes stand in greater renown than thinkers or poets. After describing the attributes of the greet athlete, he complains:

So too if he won a prize with his horses, he would obtain all these rewards, though not deserving of them as I am; for my craft (wisdom) is better than the strength of men or of horses. Yet opinion is altogether confused in this matter, and it is not right to prefer physical strength to noble Wisdom. For it is not the presence of a good boxer in the community, nor of one good at the Pentathlon or at wrestling, nor even of one who excels in fleetness of foot – which is highest in honor of all the feats of strength seen in men's athletic contests – it is not these that will give a City-State a better constitution. Small would be the enjoyment that a City-State would reap over the athletic victory of a citizen beside the banks of Pisa (Olympia). These things do not enrich the treasure-chambers of the State.

Years later, it would be Parmenides who brought fame and fortune to Elea through the wisdom of his law-giving. Notice was indeed taken of the role of wisdom. Xenophanes, then, influenced the education of young Parmenides in three important ways: first, as a poet, showing him the meaning, value and means of poetic expression. In later years, Parmenides would write his book, *On Nature*, in hexameters, with the purpose of creating divine sanction for his theme and observations. Second, Xenophanes showed the way toward unity and monotheism, a road which Parmenides would follow to its end in his vision of Being. And third, Xenophanes set the standard for the honorable life of service to the *polis*. These influences were, however, superficial, at least to the extent of being overt training. Molding the inner life would be the task of the Pythagorean, Ameinias.

Pythagoras died in Metapontum, in 497 BCE, when Parmenides was nearing his manhood and Xenophanes still his teacher. Ameinias, a disciple of Pythagoras, came along later. Undoubtedly he had been taught directly by the master in Croton, a thriving city-state on the heel of the Italian boot. The Pythagorean Brotherhood became a diaspora after the master's death, with individuals and small groups settling wherever they could find a welcome, or even tolerant acceptance. We know, for example that it was Xenophanes who reported that when Pythagoras was passing by as a dog was being whipped, "he took pity and said, 'Stop, do not beat it; for it is the soul of a friend that I recognized when I heard it giving tongue.'" So, in Elea at the time there existed something of a sympathetic environment for the mystic teachings of the master.

Reincarnation, although credited to the Hindus and Egyptians, was also part of the beliefs of the peoples of Asia Minor, particularly in Anatolia. The Orphic followers of Dionysos believed that each human being possessed a spark of divinity left over from the dismemberment of their god by the envious Titans. This belief in an immortal soul formed the Orphic beliefs of the eastern mystery religions and influenced Pythagoras as well, who combined Orphic themes with his own more exhaustive scientific studies. The combination of rigorous examination of the physical world and the attractive beliefs of Orphism drew thousands of devotees to his movement.

The basic doctrines and many tales of miracles and tangible practices confirm that Pythagoras was a seer and a guru in the best sense of that term. His followers were legion, even though the discipline endured by them was severe. No evidence exists that would suggest that a viable Pythagorean brotherhood formed in Elea, however. Most likely, Ameinias was on his own, or else he lived with a few others and Parmenides became his student in matters of astronomy, mathematics, and music.

What we do know is that Pythagorean beliefs were compatible with the Orphic mysteries during the Archaic period and that these beliefs were held in Elea. The immortality of the human soul, the transmigration of that soul through animal and human incarnations, and the journey of the soul through the cosmos to seek out its destiny, were all commonly connected beliefs. How these beliefs and practices impacted on Parmenides can be intimated from the fragments, but only intimated. We can, however, look more broadly at the pervasive influences in Mediterranean spirituality.

In the Archaic period, the cults of the Earth Mother, particularly as celebrated in the interior of Thrace and Phrygia (Anatolia), involved initiatory rituals in caves and wild places, where Bacchantes (female participants in the rites of Dionysos) were let loose from their societal constraints in order to achieve earthly forgetfulness and union with the divine. These rites were balanced in great measure by the more traditional worship of Apollo at larger sanctuaries of Delphi and Delos, as well as at local sites in each city.

In addition to the Bacchantes in wild places, men sought visions and insight through ritualized incubation in caves, where they were guided by special priests into the mysteries of the underworld. Initiates were carefully introduced into these spaces, usually feet first through small openings, and they remained for a period of hours, and in some cases days (usually nine). If they were fortunate, they saw visions, experienced transcendence, and emerged transformed. The imagery in these descriptions echoes the birthing process, an early example of what we now see in evangelical circles as being born again.

It is argued by anthropologists, of course, that the ritualization of cave incubation was an evolutionary memory from prehistory, before the period of settlement, when hunter/gatherers found caves places of safety and warmth. We need only think of those famous prehistoric cave paintings to imagine the visions and ceremonies which must have informed the lives of earlier peoples in these spaces. But enough evidence now exists to urge another interpretation of the practice. In the traditions of Thrace, Crete and the Anatolian highlands, the cave served as part of the initiatory rituals of manhood and leadership. Time spent alone in a cave stripped away the excesses of palace life, gave an opportunity for personal reflection, not to mention some peace and quiet, along with measured resolve and endurance. In Crete, for example, the king was expected to spend nine days in a cave every nine years, as a pre-condition to serving another nine years as king. Native American vision quests had a similar purpose without the severe restriction to include caves. Solitude, however, was crucial.

In areas where the Earth Mother cults were prominent, caves served as the womb of Earth, and time spent alone there, in the dark, lying quite still and awake, listening perhaps to the murmuring of underground streams, served as a transition between the human and the divine realms. The question, of course, is what was the nature of such transitional experiences? We know, for example, that the incubatory practices in Archaic medicine, as recorded in great detail at sites such as Epidauros in Greece, induced many bodily and psychic cures. But this process of incubation, which took place overnight in the Abaton (a special sleeping facility designed like a stoa) attended by the priests and snakes of Asklepios, was more of a purging of toxic energies and influences than it was a philosophical transmission of Truth. Perhaps the key lay in the time spent in incubation.

As we shall see in the fragments, the young Parmenides, whose desire takes him on the Way of Truth, travels into higher realms out of the darkness of the underworld – away from the fearsome world of dreams – and into the realm of universal light, the realm of the stars, the realm of reason. It is this imagery that suggests that Parmenides was seeking to integrate all of the sources of knowledge and wisdom of his education into a vision of unity. He was not satisfied or convinced that the everyday world of ordinary experience was the sole aspect of reality, while the underworld represented by rituals of incubation represented another, and the world of astronomy, the Royal Art, a separate world of spirit. There must be integration, and this process of integration formed the structure of his own self-transformation.

As I shall attempt to demonstrate in later chapters, Parmenides was one who, being exposed to the full range of conflicting and contrasting realities, undertook to resolve those seemingly antagonistic visions and to present in his poem a way through the contradictions. His was not an easy task, but he seemed to have accomplished it with great care and patience, given his reputation throughout Hellas.

Indeed, so great was his influence that a century later, Plato incorporated the symbolism of the cave into the Republic as part of his search for the absolute Truth, or the Good. In his imagery, the seeker is released from the cave of illusions (the *doxa* of ignorance) by his own desire (the *eros* of the seeker) and he emerges into the light of day on his way to an even greater perception of reality to come. The key to Plato's allegory is that the vision thus acquired was not local or personal but universal. Ignorance is local and personal. As Heraclitus wisely, said, *"It is necessary, therefore, to obey the universal; but although the Logos is universal, most people act as though they had a private understanding."*[3] It is private understanding that results in dualistic thinking and psychic separation.

We return now to a consideration of what the young Parmenides might have learned from his teacher Ameinias. Recall that years later, Parmenides erected a monument to his teacher, an act of profound respect and admiration. Here was a poor farmer, a Pythagorean by training and inclination, working with the son of a prominent citizen. What did they talk about? Why did Parmenides admire this teacher more than he did the famous Xenophanes?

Pythagoras had studied the phenomena of number, music and astronomy in order to discover the universal laws which lay behind them. He concluded from his investigations that these laws were further represented in reality by defining principles in the form of number that if understood properly revealed the ultimate nature of things. The guiding principles which for years had governed the construction of temples, the notes of sacred music, and the movement of the planets were the universal principles he discovered.

Parmenides would also have learned from Ameinias about the reasons Pythagoras had to leave Croton and disband the brotherhood. He would have learned that Cylon, one of the leading figures in Croton, wanted to join the brotherhood but was turned down by Pythagoras as being temperamentally unsuited to the work. Cylon took revenge on the cult by banishing it from Croton, forcing Pythagoras to move to Metapontum, where he died.

Parmenides knew that the truth of reality could not be served by creating a climate of distrust or by establishing a cult that could be susceptible to banishment. Truth, after all, should not be confused with politics or religion, as the life and death of Socrates and, later, Jesus, would illustrate. The case of Pythagoras was similar. Here were people devoting themselves to truth and to a spiritual way of life, only to have their practices condemned by outsiders whose way of life was obviously threatened by pious example. Better to work alone, Parmenides reasoned, and remain dedicated to the well-being of the community at large. In that sense, philosophy became the means by which the seeker of truth was permitted to participate in the polis and still be left alone.

The Mature Parmenides

It is not difficult to imagine – or even presume – that when he reached maturity, Parmenides had to make a critical decision as to what view of reality was most compatible with his own growing understanding. Roughly, he had two choices, at least in terms of a cosmology. The first was Hesiod's, a Genesis-like account of God's creation of the world and all the creatures in it, including humankind. In Hesiod's mythology, the gods figure prominently, and his was the traditional and accepted account among ordinary Hellenes. The second view for Parmenides was essentially Pythagorean and centered on the primacy of number as the formative force of creation.

Perhaps the best description of this view was set down by Alexander Polyhistor, who wrote a brief outline of his understanding of Pythagoreanism in the first century, BCE. He said,

> The first principle of all things is the One. From the One came an Indefinite Two, as matter for the One, which is the cause. From the One and the Indefinite Two came numbers, points; from points lines; from lines, plane figures; from plane figures, solid figures; from solid figures, sensible bodies. The elements of these are four: fire, water, earth, air; these change and are wholly transformed, and out of them comes to be a cosmos, animate, intelligent, spherical, embracing the central earth, which is itself spherical and inhabited round about.[4]

The relevance of this passage to Parmenides is its suggestion that the cosmos is presented as animate, that it is generated from a more abstract unity, as opposed to being generated by a creator god, and that the sequence of manifestation was progressive and uniform in structure. Ameinias probably communicated these principles to the young Parmenides, who accepted the basic premise of it. Those who argue that Parmenides rejected the Pythagorean view are, at the core, mistaken. He may well have rejected details and implications, but not the central premise.

The other implication arising from the Polyhistor piece is the initial passage from the One to the Indefinite Two. This view is also shared by Advaita (*Not Two*) yoga among the Indian thinkers of the same period and refined later by Shankara. The One becomes the Two when Being (Brahman) becomes conscious of itself. This self-consciousness creates the Indefinite Two, which because it is unstable results almost immediately in the Three, the Triad, which in turn creates the first stability among forces. The Four emerges naturally as the manifest creation in three dimensions, the cosmos, and is geometrically represented by the square, which represents materialization.

In the Pythagorean language of geometry, as we see above, the One is a point, the Two a line, the Three a plane, a circle or triangle, and then Four, represented by the square, which in turn grows into three dimensional structures, such as the cube. Parmenides would be primarily concerned with the nature of the One in its role as progenitor of the Many. His great leap was to suggest that the solid cosmos with which we are familiar was not the model for Being, the nature of which was not visible substance. The question then becomes, for Parmenides, whether the One is the only unity or does that unity "include" the cosmos?

The Pythagorean corpus went on from these principles to describe every aspect of reality in great detail, drawing broad principles from the laws of number. It was this broadening of principle that Heraclitus found unacceptable when he was reputed to have said that much learning was a dangerous thing, implying that learning for its own sake had drawn Pythagoras away from the truth of reality into an untenable system, which in turn deflected Pythagoras from describing accurately the nature of the manifest world. Pythagoras was not the first scientist to become absorbed in the work and to forget why he became a scientist in the first place. But, then, since Pythagoras never wrote anything down, he may well have remained focused on the problem of the transformation, or elucidation, of being.

If, however, he had stayed with principle, he might have explored in greater depth the implications of the relation between the One, Two and Three, leaving the rest to others. The idea of the point, by definition, does not exist in space/time. When the point "moves" in space/time, it must by definition form a line; it becomes Two. Space/time, then, is the equivalent of self-consciousness in the Advaita tradition by being associated with existence as an entity in space and time. The Two, however, once extant, is unstable in that it can continue extending in space/time with nothing to stop it. Its very instability creates the necessity for the third force to come into being. The Three results from the creation of the third point, creating a triangular plane and thus also creating stability. The points cease their movement, with forces working in both directions along the three lines making up the triangle.

But of course, these three forces are not in their essence stable either, and the result of their instability in space/time creates depth as the dimensions expand to articulate new forms. And since there is nothing to stop multiplicity from growing in a rampant manner, it does. In effect, every niche is filled, every possible form is articulated.

An example of this pattern in the macrocosm would be the presence of the moon in its orbit around the earth. The account most commonly accepted now is that during the formation of the planets, a meteorite or similar object struck the newly forming Earth, breaking off a large chunk of mantle, which hurtled off into space before being captured by the earth's gravity. There it remained in orbit, gradually rounding into its present shape and spin. In effect, the one (earth) became the indefinite two (the hurtling moon), which in turn became stabilized by a third force (gravity). The Big Bang took place in a similar pattern of expansion from the One to the Many (or diversity of the universe), with a resulting stability permitting order amid the chaos.

The problem is that at the more cosmic level of Being, how does One become Two in the first place. What causes Being to become aware of itself and become two? Parmenides would focus his attention on this question throughout his life – at least if we can extrapolate from the fragments (early in his life) to the conversation he has with Socrates in Plato's "Parmenides." We shall see more of this argument in Chapter 3 as we wrestle with these questions. In the meantime, though, the question remains, if all is One, how came there to be Two and then a universe? In one sense, the question seems unimportant in that its answer needn't give us pause in our daily rounds, but the question does ask about the nature of reality. Is there Being at the still point of the turning world? What is its nature? Do we receive our consciousness from Being or the evolution of the universe? Is consciousness primary or epiphenomenon?

We are brought in a circle to fragment 4:

See clearly with the mind how
Things far and near are one;

No matter how dispersed, Being
Does not separate from Being.

Santillana translates that fragment as follows: "Grasp firmly with thy mind the near and far together...this is truly the Be-er."[5] The awkward "be-er" is a way of dealing with the Greek word 'eon' in that context. Presumably, it is trying to deal with the idea of "one who creates being." For Parmenides the question was always how to translate *Eon* into language his contemporaries (and later, we) could grasp. If Plato's "Parmenides" is any indication of the struggle, it would be tough. The problem, of course, is to coordinate the poem of Parmenides with Plato's rather free-wheeling dialogue composed many years later, in which another purpose comes into play.

Death and Honors

Of the end of the life of Parmenides, we have no record, an absence which argues for normalcy. He probably died some time after 450 BCE back home in Elea. We know he was honored and that his status increased after his death, establishing the standard, "A Parmenidean Life." In 1962 a tablet was found on the site of the ancient town, saying *Parmenides, son of Pyres, Ouliades Physikos*. An *Ouliades Physikos* would have been either a physician in the traditional sense in which Hippocrates was a practicing physician, or it might have meant something more esoteric, such as "natural healer," or shaman. *Physikos* may mean nothing more than natural philosopher, in which case *Ouliades* may refer to a local cult in which Parmenides was a leader or guardian of ritual items or a leader of ceremonies. But the likelihood is that he was regarded by the Eleans as a highly respected healer/philosopher to the whole community and subsequently, they hoped, to the Hellenic world at large.

In any case, the relation between philosophy and healing is clear enough, and Parmenides would certainly have to be regarded as one who worked with committed individuals or pupils to frame a sound view of the cosmos. In other words, we cannot be truly healthy if we have a warped vision of the universe or a warped vision of human nature. If a human being is to be whole, he or she must be of sound mind, and a sound mind has as much to do with a rich, expansive vision of the universe as it does with how we approach the ordinary challenges of each day. Clearly Parmenides had such a sound, expansive vision and was indeed fortunate in his life.

CHAPTER 2 - THE FRAGMENTS

PARMENIDES WROTE A long poem entitled "On Nature." We have several fragments of the poem, preserved by later historians, philosophers and commentators. Two-thirds, possibly more, is lost. We know a little more about the whole, fortunately, from Plato's dialogue "Parmenides," which describes a visit by the aging philosopher to Athens, where he meets with interested intellectuals, including a young Socrates. A small industry of interpretation has evolved out of the complexity of Plato's dialogue, leading to varied conclusions about the missing sections. But, more of that below.

The "Nature"of the title is the Greek *physis* [foo-sis], a term that expresses a visionary concern for "the nature of things," not just the tangible facts of physical nature. It appears, in fact, that most Presocratic truth-seekers expressed their views in a similar way, entitling their work "On Nature" as a sign that they were not writing a poem entitled "On the Gods." *Physis* was the general topic, and each thinker made a contribution, some in more abstract language than others. That Parmenides chose the verse form was also an accepted means of expression, following Hesiod and, to some extent, Homer. Verse was the language of revelation. The rhythm and sound of the hexameters[6] elevated thought above ordinary discourse. In more recent times, we have the example of Shakespeare, who employed prose in his plays only for fools and madmen. Iambic pentameter was reserved for rational (albeit sometimes brutal) discourse.

It is also useful to remember that the Greeks spoke their verse aloud. Silent reading was unknown until the Roman era. The eye followed the unbroken line of letters, the words rolled off the tongue, were caught by the ear, and only then could meaning be grasped by the understanding. Since Greek is an inflected language, word order depends on sound, how the words flow together, how vowels and consonants combine to produce a smooth, harmonic measure. As a result, the hard consonants do not bump into one another. A vowel invariably intercedes to smooth the way. Word order then, is based on auditory effect, not grammar, and meaning arises as much from this effect as from the vocabulary, making translation into English a challenge, especially from poetry to poetry. Poetic licence is required, even encouraged.

As flawed as the following transliterated verse is, it is a serious attempt to capture both the sound and sense of Parmenidean revelation, which is what his poem was meant to be. The result, hopefully, is revealed truth, arrived at in communion with divine communion, at least insofar as Parmenides experienced it. The poem emerges from the force of Persuasion, the goddess who keeps company with Justice, whose task it is to guard the gates giving access to the realm of higher knowledge. The youth, or *kouros*, gains admittance to this realm through his desire for truth and comes from the strength of *eros* in his soul. It is access that anyone who is worthy and who deeply desires such communion can attain. On the basis of what is traditionally called the 'proem,' his journey into the cosmos to the goddess, we are asked to accept that Parmenides was granted admittance to a special realm and once in the presence of divinity, received the Way of Truth.

Fragments of **On Nature** by Parmenides

The Proem

1.[7]

The mares carry my chariot, the goddesses leading the way,
As far as my desire can reach along the celebrated road
That bears the one who knows throughout the broad world.
The horses, the bright, eager mares, draw the chariot along,
The glowing axle yields a high piping song,
As it whirls in the naves, driven by the spinning wheels.
The maidens, daughters of the Sun, leaving the depths of Night
Quicken their pace in the direction of the Light,
Now throw back the veils from their heads.

There in the halls of Darkness are the gates of Day and Night,
Closed in by a lintel above, a threshold below, with heavy doors
Where avenging Justice holds firm the mighty bolts.
The skillful maidens, murmuring their pleading words,
Prevail on Justice to draw back the bar without delay.
The fine-wrought bronze gives way to the abyss

And the great doors fly open, pivoting in their sockets,
And straight through on the broad road the maidens drive.

*   *   *

The goddess receives me with kind words;
Taking my right hand in hers, she addresses me:
"Youth, attended as you are by immortal ones,

Brought here by the mares to my dwelling place,
Welcome! No evil destiny has drawn you here,
So very far from human habitation.

It is by divine command and right that you have come.
You shall inquire into everything, into the vast unmoving
Heart of well-rounded Truth, and also into the opinions
Of mortals, where Truth cannot reside. Even so,
You will learn opinion as well, to move through
Those things that merely seem, to learn to test them.

2.
Come now, I will tell you all there is to know;
You will possess the word when you have heard it:
These ways to know are alone to be considered....
[lost material]

*   *   *

The Way of Truth

First, know that It Is, and it is not possible
For Is not to be. This is the way of Persuasion,
Who dwells with Truth. Next, the other, that It Is Not,
Cannot be. That is a path not to tread upon.
You cannot know what is Not, nor speak about it.

3.
What is there for thinking and for being is the same.

4.

See clearly with the mind how
Things far and near are one;
No matter how dispersed, Being
Does not separate from Being.

5.

It matters not at all where I begin;
I will return again to the same place.

*　　　　*　　　　*

6.

It is wise both to say and to think that Being is.
For to be is there to be, and nothingness is not;
Consider carefully and bar your thought from
The ordinary way that mortals take: of two minds,
Knowing nothing, wandering aimlessly in thought,
Swept along, as deaf as blind, dazed, an unwitting herd.

7,8

For them, To Be and Not To Be are just the same;
For them, all things subsist in back-bending strain.
Never must you come to think that Nothingness can be,
Never follow this way of seeking after truth,
Nor let ordinary habits compel your chosen path.

Never allow the sightless eye to rule, the sound-congested ear,
The chattering tongue, but let highest Reason judge
The oft-contested proof I here provide to you....

*   *   *

Only one account of the Way remains: Being Is!
Along this path are many signs: Being is uncreated,
Eternal, Whole, of only one substance, unmoved
And without end.....

Nor can we say it Was or it Will Be,
Because It Is Now, Whole, One, Continuous.
What birth can you find for it, what coming-to-be?
Nor may you speak of Being arising from Nothing,
For Nothingness has no words or cohering thought.

If born, what necessity brought it forth?
Was it made in the past or in more recent times?
Did it grow from Nothing? This cannot be.
It must exist absolutely or not exist at all.
Justice will never loose her bonds
To allow It to come to be or cease to be.

Instead she holds it fast. It has been decided:
Either It Is or It Is Not. The resolution has been made.
Necessity demands that one way be unthought
And inexpressible. The other is the way of Being.
So how could Being perish? How could it come to be?
If somehow it came to be, then it is Not.

Nor can It come to be in some future time.
Thus, coming-to-be and dying are unheard of.

*   *   *

Nor can Being be divided, since it is all One.
Nor can It be dissolved, to become a lesser thing,
But all things are full of Being and continuous.
For Being holds Being close in powerful bonds,
Without beginning or ending, because Becoming
And Extinction have been driven far away.
True conviction has sent them far away.

Remaining always the same, Being rests
By itself, staying firmly fixed, for Necessity,
Full of power, holds it in the grip of Limits,
Surrounding it, prescribed by divine law
That Being shall not be without bounds
Though lacking nothing, being without limit,
It would thus be lacking everything.

*　　　*　　　*

To think is the same as the thought, It Is.
Thinking cannot subsist without Being,
It lives in all that can been said.
There is nothing that can or shall be
But Being itself, for Necessity holds it firm
To remain entire and without change.

Therefore, all things that mortals have set forth
Believing them all to be true, are merely names:
Becoming, Perishing, Being and Not-Being,
Alterations in all the bright hues of the world.

As for Being, since there is limit, complete

On every side, like the form of a perfect sphere,
Symmetrical from its center in all directions,
Not bound to be more or less to any span,
Nor bound by Not-Being from reaching out,
It flows out, equal to itself, to form a whole.

*   *   *

The Way of Opinion [the change to prose]

Now I cease my truthful words concerning well-rounded Truth, and from this point on you must learn the opinions of the mortal world by listening to the deceptive order of my words – or the order of my deceptive words.

Mortals established the custom of dividing things in two, as opposite in form. They distinguished one from the other through signs. On the one hand, there is the flaming fire of the heavens, gentle, light in weight, and the same in every direction. It is not the same as the other.

This other, also unique and opposite, is dark night, a dense and heavy body. I describe this world-order to you as it seems to be, with all its phenomena, so that no clever mortal can out-think you.

9.
Thus, since all things are divided into Light and Night, and names have been doled out to each class of thing according to their power, all things are full of either Light or Night, as both are equal because neither has any share of the other.

10.

You shall study the nature of the heavens, with all the constellations, also the powerful force of the bright sun, and from whence they all came into being. And you shall study the wandering nature of the moon, as well as the surrounding heavens, from whence it came to be and how Necessity contrived to bind the wandering of the stars.

11.

I will tell you how the earth, sun and moon, the space common to them all, the Milky Way in the heavens, even outermost Olympus, and the searing power of the stars sped into being.

12.

The narrower rings were mixed with undiluted Fire, the next with black Night, but in between rushed the measure of Flame. At the center is the goddess who steers all things. It is she who governs cruel birth and intercourse, bringing male and female, and female and male to mingle together.

13.

First of all the gods she fashioned Love.

14, 15 (On the moon)

Shining in the Night with light not her own, wandering around the earth, always gazing at the sun.

16.

In the same measure as the various rambling limbs possessed by each individual, so too with the mind. It is the constitution which thinks, and thinking is governed by excess.

17.

On the right boys, on the left girls.... (context and order uncertain)

18.

When male and female mix their seed together in love, the force that shapes the child in the veins, from different blood, can mold a well-proportioned body only if it holds a proper measure. If the forces are in conflict when the seed is joined, and they fail to make a unity, the resulting conflict will plague the growing fetus.

*　　　*　　　*

1. Commentary on The Proem

The Archaic world of 500 BCE was just beginning to fade when Parmenides was nearing maturity. The Hellenic world was a myth-o-poetic culture in crisis. Change and chaos were in the air, and only the slow, predictable heavens provided stability. Whatever it was that the inhabitants of small city-states knew about the relationship of the trembling earth beneath their feet to the sun, moon, five known planets and stars above them, was learned and passed on from observation. The heavens revolved around their fixed place in regular, predictable motions, from day to day, year to year and lifetime to lifetime. And beyond that, astronomers passed on to one another, from generation to generation, the great cycles marking ages.

The dome of the sky appeared to turn around a fixed point, the north star, which was worshiped as an earth/sky goddess, one of the attributes of Demeter/Persephone. This still point of the turning world was thus a source of spiritual attention and devotion. The Milky Way, the edge of our galaxy seen edge on, was to these observers the Royal Road through the cosmologic landscape, a broad white path from one world to another, a connection to the Beyond, the *apeiron*.

The young Parmenides must have spent many evening hours with his teacher Ameinias examining the night sky. Lying on the bluff overlooking the sea, the two sky-watchers would have had nearly a 360-degree horizon to study. Half the horizon was the sea, a wonderful guide to the rising and setting of constellations. Behind them, to the East, the soft hills veiled for a time the rising sun and morning stars. It was in this way, from the Pythagoreans, that Parmenides was exposed to the "music of the spheres," the *mousike* of the Greek cultural consciousness.

Perhaps the best expression of this Archaic consciousness and how cosmology, religion, and philosophy were gathered into a unity comes from the Bhagavad Gita, part of the Mahabharata set down in the seventh century BCE in the East. In this relevant section of Book VIII, The Lord Shri Krishna explains to Arjuna the relationship between the movements of the cosmos and the times propitious for human transcendence.

> *Now I will tell thee, O Arjuna, of the times at which, if the mystics go forth they do not return, and at which they go forth only to return.*

> *If knowing the Supreme Spirit the sage goes forth with fire and light, in the daytime, in the fortnight of the waxing moon and*

in the sixth months before the Northern summer solstice, he will attain the Supreme.

But if he departs in gloom, at night, during the fortnight of the waning moon and in the sixth months before the Southern solstice, then he reaches but lunar light and he will be born again.[8]

From this imagery we understand that the solstices were soul-gates, points of entry which the knowing soul could travel, through the gates of Night and Day, and the north-south axis stood as a pillar guarded by the figure of Justice. These connections to Parmenides were admirably set down in a 1964 essay by Giorgio de Santillana entitled "The Way of Clarity."

Santillana cites Plutarch's judgment that Parmenides was more a naturalist than a mystic and that he was describing in the Proem a coherent, unified cosmos in which human beings had a place and a reason for being. In the scheme of the naturalist, then, Being encompasses the entire system, and using the terminology of Pythagoras, the geometry of space. If human beings wish to know "The Way of the Gods," they must look to the heavens, where the movements of the planets through the slow, deliberate movement of the stars symbolized Olympian participation in human affairs but more important, where the consistency of the heavenly movements denoted coherence and order.

Rather than feeling alienated by the awesome expanse of the universe, Parmenides and his teacher Ameinias must have felt at one with the night sky, attuned to its predictable movements from season to season and year to year. Today, deafened as we are by our so-called technological wonders, we cannot "hear" the music of the spheres. We understand visually through the mind-shattering reaches of the Hubble telescope that we spin through the cosmos at frightening speeds, that we exist somewhere on the fringes of a galaxy with 400 billion stars in it and that billions of galaxies, some much larger than our own, are speeding away from us at alarming rates. And knowing that these galaxies are speeding away faster and faster only adds to our vertigo.

How do we react to this "situation?" The first thing we do is to reject all "ancient" observations and beliefs as naive, as irrelevant. "They knew so little, these ancient ones," we say. "We know better now. Such is progress." But what is it, exactly, that we know now about how it all come to be that they did not? Very little of substance. We forget that their accurate and relevant vision of the movement of the heavens stood as a symbol of Being, but not as Being itself. Polaris wasn't a god, but a correspondence of stillness. "Being is like that," the ancients said, pointing to the north star. It appears in Parmenides' poem in fragment twelve as "the goddess who steers all things." That is a deception, of course, but it expresses the principle, once again, of the still point of the turning world, the axis of Being.

For example, Santillana points out the precision of the symbolic imagery in writing about how Parmenides employed astronomical features.

> In the field of astronomy, Parmenides is said to have taught the division of the sphere of the earth into regions corresponding to the celestial circles marked by equator and tropics, and indeed, if we are to believe Theophrastus, it is he and not Pythagoras who first taught that the earth is round. He is also said by Diogenes Laertius to have identified the morning and the evening star as one and the same planet. These could hardly have been called discoveries in one or the other region of

the Mediterranean World, but in Greece, still under the spell of Ionion Physics, they put Parmenides in the forefront of mathematikoi. His contemporaries might well have referred to him, as Socrates says of Timaeus, as 'the astronomikotos of us all.'[9]

It is no matter that we no longer use the laws of celestial mechanics as symbolic representations of the Divine. In our own time, following the trends of philosophy and psychology, we have internalized the Divine into our own consciousness, making Mind as *Higher Consciousness* a central symbol of connection to the eternal. In Greek history, that step took place during the Classical crisis with Anaxagoras, but more of that later.

Rather than reject the Parmenidean symbolism in the Proem as archaic and thus irrelevant to our present level of awareness, we might instead reconnect to the celestial dynamics, even to the point of reacquainting ourselves with the movements of stars and planets. And I do not mean astrology, at least as its mundane versions as practiced in our popular culture. Through most of history, astrology has been used as a prophetic tool to determine human destiny and not as a source of understanding of divine presence or what Plato called "the moving image of eternity." But combined with astronomy, the Royal Art, astrology described the broad movements of history and overall human destiny from age to age.

If, for example, the earth's motion on its axis was perfect, that is, without any noticeable wobble, the north star (currently Polaris), would forever be the still point of the turning world as far as we (Earthlings) are concerned. It would be the fixed place in the universe, Being itself. But even the ancients knew better. The earth, as it happens, wobbles like a top. As a result, the north/south axis turns in a slow circle of approximately 23 degrees, pulled by the sun's gravitation, in a full cycle every 25,920 years. This motion is called the Precession. As a result of this gyroscopic movement, the sun meets the equator on the vernal equinox at a point which shifts slowly through the zodiac. Recorded history has witnessed about a quarter of this movement, or about 6,600 years.

Thus, over that period we have moved from Taurus, into Aries, into Pisces and, soon, into Aquarius. The movement into Pisces took place in 6 BCE, corresponding to the birth of Christ, hence the symbol of the fish to denote early Christianity. The very slowness of the Precession helped to affirm the conscious movement of eternity through human history, thus bringing coherence to the movement of the ages. Even today, much has been made of the coming Age of Aquarius as a new era in human destiny.[10] We are not immune to this symbolism.

To repeat, the variations in the earth's movements, the relative permanence of Polaris, the succession of Ages and the constancy of the annual cycles, all worked together to connect the perfect stillness of Divine nature to the order of human existence by creating a spectrum of gradual change, from very slow (the ages of the Precession), to the annual rites of the solstices and equinoxes. How did the ancients steady themselves in the chaos of existence? They looked up and counted, whereas we look inward, still the mind and meditate on the still point.

The Corpus Hermeticum

It is difficult in our postmodern disjunctures to convey the purity of vision contained in the Parmenidean fragments without leaping to deconstruction. A comparison of lesser light might be useful to gradually return to the sense of ancient authority. Certain similarities exist between the poem of Parmenides and the Corpus Hermeticum, particularly that most famous section, *Libellus I*, in which the youthful seeker is taken up to the realm of Poimandres, Mind of the Sovereignty, there to inquire into the nature of things. The scene is similar in imagery to the youthful Parmenides entering the realm of the goddess to learn similar truths and may indeed have been influenced by the earlier poem.

The following excerpt from the *Hermeticum* is the relevant passage:

> *Once on a time, when I had begun to think about the things that are, and my thoughts had soared high aloft, while my bodily senses had been put under restraint by sleep, – yet not such sleep as men weighed down by fullness of food or by bodily weariness – methought there came to me a Being of vast and boundless magnitude, who called me by my name, and said to me, "What do you wish to hear and see, and to learn and come to know by thought?" "Who are you," I said. "I," said he, "am Poimandres, the Mind of the Sovereignty. "I would fain learn," said I, "the things that are and understand and their nature and get knowledge of God. These," said I, "are the things of which I wish to hear." He answered, "I*

know what you wish for; indeed I am with you everywhere; keep in mind all you desire to learn and I will teach you."

When he had thus spoken, forthwith all things changed in aspect before me and were opened out in a moment. And I beheld a boundless view; all was change into light, a mild and joyous light and I marveled when I saw it and in a little while, there had come to be in one part a downward-tending darkness, terrible and grim...and thereafter I saw the darkness changing into watery substance, which was unspeakably tossed about, and gave forth smoke as from fire; and I heard it making an indescribable sound of lamentation; for there was sent forth from it an inarticulate cry. But from the Light there come forth a holy Word, which took its stand upon the watery substance; and methought this Word was the voice of the Light.

And Poimandres spoke for me to hear, and said to me: "Do you understand the meaning of what you have seen?" "Tell me its meaning," I said, "and I shall know." "That Light," he said, "is I, even Mind, the first God, who was before the watery substance which appeared out of the darkness; and the Word which came forth from the Light is son of God." "How so?" said I. "Learn my meaning," said he,"by looking at what you yourself have in you; for in you too, the Word is son, and the mind is father of the word. They are not separate from one another; for life is the union of word and mind."[11]

The first and most obvious relation between the two passages lies in their introductory images. In the Parmenides, we are taken on a chariot ride in the Archaic myth-o-poetic transport reserved for the Olympian gods. We are swept through the regions of Darkness to the gates of Night and Day where Justice (Dike) guards the doors. The essential "rightness" of the young man's quest opens those doors and admits him to the inner sanctum, where the goddess takes his right hand (a literal symbol of truth) in hers and offers assurance and a welcome. She begins right away to convey her *logos*, the abiding account of divine reality and the subsequent road to the Truth. In this case, Reality and Truth are the same, are One, and Justice is the guardian of the Way to that unity.

In the Hermeticum, on the other hand, Mind explains things in language much more familiar to human intellectual reasoning. We learn the relation between the Word (also the *Logos*) and God the father, the familiar beginning to the Gospel of John. Mind also says "You have seen in your mind the archetypal form, which is prior to the beginning of things, and is limitless." Here is a similar image to the description of the nature of Being, but with the distinct difference that a label – archetypal form – has been supplied as a point of reference. That label sets up a duality in the expression, a distancing from the purity of knowing. The condition is given a name, a practice which the goddess explains in Parmenides is part of the mortal view of things.

The major difference between the Parmenides and the *Hermiticum* is the difference between what is unfamiliar and familiar, between unity and duality. It is the difference between a revelation of a new paradigm and an account of what is already familiar. We hardly understand the former because unity of mind is very nearly unfathomable to us. And yet, this vision of unity is the central message of the goddess, which she expresses as a unity, rather than talking *about* unity. We have no language for this vision other than images of Eastern enlightenment. We might say, for example, "All Is!" as a way of fighting our way into the idea, but we are blocked at the grammatical gate by laws of syntax and agreement. All things (*ta panta*) is the Greek expression for multiplicity. *To en* is an expression of unity, The One. We might say, then, *ta panta en*, thus crashing or crunching the syntax together into a new meaning of the relationship between One and All. But we can't.

Aside from the decidedly Christian overtones of the *Hermeticum* and the seven hundred year gap between the two texts, (the dating of the Hermeticum is uncertain) the other major difference lies in the kind of language used, particularly by the divine figure. The goddess in Parmenides speaks very differently. Hers is the language of unity, whereas Poimandres speaks in the ordinary way of mortals. The difference is not merely a matter of translation either. The goddess speaks differently, both in tone and in kind from the later source. Hers is the sound of unity.

Hesiod

Those curious to know where and how Parmenides came to his 'vision' – for surely it was one – have several choices. The first, and most rational answer, is tradition, and tradition in Archaic Greece means Hesiod and the Homeric authors of the *Iliad and Odyssey*. The form of the Proem most closely follows Hesiod and his invocation of the Heliconian Muses in the very first line of his *Theogony*. These three ancient figures represent meditation (*Melete*), remembrance (*Mneme*) and song (*Aoide*). The maidens who accompany the youth on the Way may well be these Muses, who in the personification of meditation, remembrance, and song form a triad leading to spiritual knowledge and inspiration. They represent in Hesiod the medium through which the gods transmit divine knowledge to mortals.

But here the connection to Hesiod ceases. In the *Theogony* Hesiod is not given mystical transport to the realm of the gods. The Muses come to him in his earthly abode as he tends his flocks with others near Mt. Helicon, and what they say to them bears no resemblance to how the goddess treats the youth in the Proem. In Hesiod, the Muses say,

Listen, you country bumkins, you swag-swilling yahoos,
we know how to tell many lies that pass for truth,
and we know, when we wish, to tell the truth itself."[12]

The Muses then breathe into Hesiod the *logos* of past and future, but not the nature of Being itself. Creation is their saga and it begins with Chaos and ends with the tales of immortal goddesses who share the beds of mortal men. So we cannot find in the traditional literature of creation epics a source for Parmenides' vision of timeless/spaceless Being. In fact, there is none in Greek literature, other than Fragment 24 of Heraclitus which reads, "*This cosmos [the unity of all that is] was not made by immortal or mortal beings, but always was, is and will be an eternal fire, arising and subsiding in measure.*" We have no reason to conclude, however, that Parmenides knew the work of Heraclitus, given the distance between them. But we shall consider their work together later on.

The other crucial difference between the two proems is the way the Muses speak to Hesiod, referring to him as a 'yahoo' in this translation, a combination of a fool and an ignoramus. It seems that these Muses will not be conveying a high level of data to this incompetent mortal. For Parmenides, on the other hand, the transmission *is* at a much higher level, and it appears that he wishes to establish a contrast with what the Muses are prepared to reveal to Hesiod.

But if we consider the Heliconian Muses as a source for both transmissions, we may be able to establish what sort of experience lay behind the Parmenidean inspiration. The muses are Meditation, Memory and Song: the stilling of the active, cursive mind, the remembrance of First Things, and the harmony of the spheres. These combine to provide the source of knowledge and the means of expressing it.

The first striking image in the proem – beyond the chariot ride itself – is "the vast unmoving heart of well-rounded truth." The Greek *atremes*, literally, not-trembling, or its affirmative 'still,' is the key to the later description of Being. In meditation, the still mind comes before any experience of the *apeiron*, or Beyond. So too with the well-rounded truth, in this case the Greek word *eu-*

kukleos, literally 'well-wheeled,' in the sense of smooth, unwavering. These are indications of the *logos* to come. And just as the truth to be told is unmoving and well-rounded, so the mind of the listener must be in the same state: unagitated and steady.

It should be clear then that the Proem is primarily meant to convey an actual experience and is not merely serving a traditional Homeric trope. Parmenides was conveyed to the place of the goddess, a higher state, where he received his revelation. The vivid scene is real, the details palpable. The high-pitched whine of the axle, spinning in its naves, is redolent of the harmony of the spheres at the point that the chariot approaches the Cyclopean gates, where Justice holds the key. The blend of real and abstract also creates a harmony and prepares us for the gift to come.

The image which comes immediately to mind of the youth with the goddess is the justly famous fifth century BCE relief found at Eleusis picturing Demeter, Persephone and the youth Triptolemos [following page]. In the relief (now at the Archaeological Museum in Athens) Demeter raises her right hand and places either a seed or a chaff of wheat in the right hand of the youth, thus transferring to humanity the blessings of agriculture, or life itself.

The relief speaks to the Proem of Parmenides. The gift of life takes place from right hand to right hand. The naked youth, smaller than the goddesses, looks up. He stands, right foot forward, in the manner of an Archaic *kouros*. The goddess looks down at him kindly. Behind him, Persephone, as the virgin aspect of the Mother, holds her right hand over the youth's head in benediction. The whole relief spells harmony, love, devotion and perfection. The youth in this case is no yahoo or bumpkin, but rather a young hero, future founder of Eleusis and first priest

of Demeter there. As such he was revered as the keeper of the
Mysteries.

Fig. 1: Eleusis Relief, Demeter, Persephone and the youth Triptolemos,
fifth century BCE

2. The Way of Truth

The goddess of the Proem says, "First, know that It Is, and it is not possible/ For Is not to be." The English phrase 'It Is," only partially captures the radical nature of this cardinal message. She really says, in effect, "Know Is!" The verb form of 'to be' *esti*, has no subject in the verse. Parmenides really says "Is!" It is as if the goddess, holding the youth's hand, looks him in the eye and slowly, emphatically, speaks the word of existence itself, the word that corresponds to the biblical 'Let there be light." Most commentators render the sense of it in the word 'being,' as in "Being Is," but that choice feels more like the Hermeticum in more dualistic phrasing.[13] We understand "Being is" in somewhat the same sense as the famous biblical phrase, "I am," in which the God of Moses speaks to the people of Israel. "Tell them 'I Am' sent you." But Being is not Yahweh here, like a persona, and thus does not speak. The sense must be understood without a subject. We are trying to get at a feeling of is-ness.

In the Parmenides the text reduces grammar to pure predication, removing the subject so that no duality is allowed to creep in. Finally, after struggling with the syntax myself, I have to agree with Freeman, who renders the passage, "It is," employing as she does the indefinite pronoun used when we say, "It is raining." We realize in that case that 'it' does not have an antecedent. It is not that the weather is raining or that the rain is raining. "It is raining" simply states the case that rain is falling intransitively. We wish to express a condition rather than an action – a state of raining, as it were, or rain-ness.

In the same way, 'It Is' places the emphasis on the verb as a condition of being without establishing being as a personage, a divine being who represents what the goddess is trying to express to her young seeker. She is speaking loosely of the condition of existence without reference to living, breathing existence. She does not mean to say the universe exists with 'It Is,' or that a being exists, as in an individual being of some preeminent stature. It is simply that 'It Is,' and that Not Is cannot be. Nothingness isn't.

The next section of the Way of Truth sets down the way the "knowing man" must think about Being. This crucial section answers the questions posed by human curiosity about the nature of Being: is it a being, many beings, a conscious being? What are its, his, her or, better, *the* qualities? Xenophanes was generally right about the gods. We do in fact project our own form onto divinity? Granted, Zeus and the other Olympians do not literally sit on thrones on Mt. Olympus debating the destiny of human beings. What then are the gods? Is there God? What Is Being? Or, to put the case differently, what are the attributes of Being?

These are questions of consciousness and the expression of thought. We are aware, on occasion, that thoughts arise in mind as flashes of insight, an Aha! of awareness. At this initial stage of perception, the perception may not form itself into a thought, or precise language, or at least into grammatical syntax. It is only later that we say, "I just had a thought," when we begin the process of formatting sentences around the perception, like a basket being woven around a stone. But initially, the 'Aha" is language-free.

The goddess then tells Parmenides, "What is there for thinking and for being is the same." Here is a crucial affirmation from the goddess. She tells the youth that transcendent being is capable of apprehension through thought. Being can be known because 'Is' or Being is in some way bounded and finite, although mysteriously so. We have not been introduced to an infinite, boundless, shapeless entity, and since what *is not* cannot be, the negation cannot be thought of. Nothing is not, nor can it be conceived. At the same time, Parmenides affirms that *Nous*, or the cognitive organ of being, is capable of knowing all there is of being. The transcendent can be grasped by the *Nous* because the *Nous* is an organ of Being, just as the *Logos* is an attribute of Being as well.

A deflection into issues of translation is needed at this point. Much has been made of fragment 3, which in many translations is rendered, "For thinking and being is the same."

Therefore, the link between *logos* and being is established. The declaration, "In the beginning was the Word," (*Logos*) is a similar formulation, but with a difference. Parmenides is careful not to confine his speculation of being to the limits of time. There is no "beginning" here. Thought and Being exist eternally in his formulation, and whatever is possible for a human being to think is identical to what is possible to be because the *Nous* is a faculty of Being through which its *logos* is articulated.

The important formulation here is that *Nous* for Parmenides lies outside the narrow confines of human attribute. The *Nous*, as we will see in the Epilogue with Anaxagoras, is similar in kind to the idea of Universal Mind found in German Idealism and Emerson (the Over-Soul). Just as human beings possess a mind, so is, or does, Being. Unfortunately, Anaxagoras chose to isolate *Nous* and make it alone the unifying force of creation. Much later, modern philosophy (particularly Hegel) would make the individual human mind supreme and place being within its confines. In this reductive process, then, Being fuses into *Nous*, which in turn is reduced to human Mind in evolutionary biology. A further reduction among the positivists eliminates the troublesome word 'mind' altogether, leaving us with the objective terms of biology, chemistry and physics. We are left with "I breathe, therefore I exist." Lost then, for modern human beings, is the Parmenidean dictum, I am because Being exists.

With Parmenides the cosmos opens wide and the individual human mind, rather than being captive within its organism, partakes of the whole because it is part of the whole. The narrow aspect of human mind, therefore, is a local phenomenon allowing the knowing individual access to that whole. The point is made more clearly when the goddess says, "It matters not at all from which point I begin, / As I will return once more to the same place." Start with thinking, and being can be known. Start with being, and thinking can be known. That can only be if the cosmos is a continuum without a beginning or end, without a center or point of origin and without the limitation of time, which by its nature creates linear sequence, beginning and end.

This point becomes clearer when the goddess begins to describe some of the aspects of being.

Only one account of the Way remains: It Is!
Along this path are many signs: Being is uncreated,
Eternal, Whole, of only one substance, unmoved
And without end.....

Nor can we say it Was or it Will Be,
Because It Is Now, Whole, One, Continuous.
What birth can you find for it, what coming-to-be?
Nor may you speak of Being arising from Nothing,
For Nothingness has no words or cohering thought.

This formulation contradicts Hesiod's Theogony. The traditional view presents a created cosmos and created, semi-immortal, gods. It was a comforting notion because it fit with human perceptions of birth and death and the hope that if the gods were born and yet were immortal (to a point), so too might human destiny somehow be the same. Parmenides shatters this simplicity by establishing an eternal Being in a continuum of which a created cosmos appears. This latter formulation resulted in viewing Parmenides as a dualistic thinker, positing two separate realities. That the goddess asserts a vision of unity becomes clearer as the "teaching" continues.

> *If born, what necessity brought it forth?*
> *Was it made in the past or in more recent times?*
> *Did it grow from Nothing? This cannot be.*
> *It must exist absolutely or not exist at all.*
> *Justice will never loose her bonds*
> *To allow It to come to be or cease to be.*

The logic of this argument is unassailable, at least in the terms presented. If Nothingness is defined as Not Being, then something cannot emerge from it, and it cannot be said to exist. Similarly, then, Being must exist absolutely. If, for example, our universe began in a single fiery explosion some fifteen billion years ago, it began out of a potential, some presence of energy existing under certain conditions. Although some physicists argue that the universe appeared out of a vacuum, that so-called vacuum was not Nothingness. It was full of potential, alternating charges out of which matter appeared.[14] How the conditions with that state "changed" in some way such as to "excite" the Big Bang is still a matter of debate among cosmologists. But something changed from an existing condition, and one would have to assume an eternal condition, since time, as we understand it, began with that explosion into matter from a source of energy.

The goddess asks the relevant question at the beginning of this section: "If born, what necessity brought it forth?" Justice (*Dike*), who bars the door to reality from those unfit to perceive it, also holds fast to the very fabric of reality itself. This is the source of unity in this vision. Justice and Necessity (*ananke*) operate at every level of existence, from Being to Nature. A wise human being understands the workings of Justice and Necessity, stern masters of the universe and human life. Within the context of life, every individual contends with what must, of necessity, take place. By the same token, reality, or being, must also abide by these rules, and the goddess uses this argument to persuade the youth that Being *must* of necessity lack nothing, be whole, undivided and eternal.

Finally, as a way of describing in some measure the qualities of being, Parmenides risks the dangers of describing attributes, but with perfect symbolic accuracy.

> *As for Being, since there is limit, complete*
> *On every side, like the form of a perfect sphere,*
> *Symmetrical from its center in all directions,*
> *Not bound to be more or less to any span,*
> *Nor bound by Not-Being from reaching out,*
> *It flows out, equal to itself, to form a whole.*

This section articulates an image of perfection and harmony in the aspect of Being. If there were no limits, the result would be formlessness and admit Not-Being. Being must have the qualities of perfection – like a perfect sphere – and it must exhibit symmetry, this because the cosmos has given us number, geometric form, and harmony. If All is One, then the One must possess the qualities of perfection.

We see this pattern in Plato's "Timaeus," where Being employs its organ Mind, the ruling power, to persuade Necessity to bring the greater part of created things to perfection, through which the universe was created (48a). The image of perfection in Parmenides appears in the sphere, the expanded point.

The mystery in this form is the absence of an edge. The "sphere" is *Not bound to be more or less to any span*, and yet it radiates out uniformly from its center, its point. But the point has no origin or implies no beginning, the way we might think of a "starting point." This image differs from the image of the *apeiron* or Beyond of other Greek thinkers in projecting a so-called center of Being that is everywhere and nowhere, unbounded, and thus unknowable.

3. The Way of Opinion

Not only does this section of the poem lack contextual unity, it is also fragmented by loss and conflicting editorial speculation. Commentators (including Aristotle) seem to have fused or confused some of the material with Parmenides' own opinion in this section as to the true nature of things. What the goddess presents in this section is the received tradition, the Homeric view, as it were. It is how we think about ourselves and about things "out there." Not only do we divide things into twos, we do not even agree on the categories to be divided. And yet, as we shall see, the description of duality presented here is natural and eventually, in its own convoluted way, provides access to Being.

The goddess declares, "*Do not believe this to be the case*: all things are divided into Light and Night..." Clever mortals will argue this view, she says, but the youth must be prepared to wipe all duality from his mind. The argument is telling. The goddess tells Parmenides not to trust the opinions she is about to relate. And yet she presents "the facts" in such a way as to make them sound convincing. And the reason for that is that they seem perfectly plausible. Rather than treat the opinions of mortals as false from the outset, she assumes the role of a philosopher extolling the virtues of duality, with the result that the argument seems true. This "seeming" will prove useful later on.

In one fragment (10) she appears to be describing the studies of the Pythagoreans.

You shall study the nature of the heavens, with all the constellations, also the powerful force of the bright sun, and from whence they all came into being. And you shall study the wandering nature of the moon, as well as the surrounding heavens, from whence it came to be and how Necessity contrived to bind the wandering of the stars.

These are scientific studies, investigations into the workings of nature for the purpose of understanding the world. Among the dubious fragments attributed to Heraclitus is one criticizing Pythagoras for being too much in the grip of worldly knowledge, of forgetting the real purpose of philosophy, which is knowledge of reality. Parmenides, too, might be offering the same warning, but thinly disguised. Or, his views might be more sympathetic, given his training from Ameinias. When we think we understand the mechanics of the universe, we run the risk of attributing our own nature to those mechanics. The result is a radical reductionism suggesting, ultimately, that human beings are merely DNA's way of making more DNA. Parmenides warned us away from this point of view two thousand, five hundred years ago.

Fragment 12 reads: *The narrower rings were mixed with undiluted Fire, the next with black Night, but in between rushed the measure of Flame. At the center is the goddess who steers all things. It is she who governs cruel birth and intercourse, bringing male and female, and female and male to mingle together.*

Here, the image of the sphere contains the finite cosmos, emanating from the will of the goddess of nature who steers all things. The mortal who is able to step back and apprehend being in the dualities of the cosmos will comprehend the truth, severing it from opinion. Undiluted Fire (in the way of Heraclitus) suggests the purity of energy from which the cosmos emerges in the image of the perfect sphere of Being itself. And the true thinker can also see the unity of the male/female interaction, which in nature is perceived only as "cruel birth and intercourse."

The point, then, of the section on opinion is that the knowing seeker is able to penetrate the illusions of duality presented by the world to the unity beneath, once shown the severe beauty of Being. But as the goddess says, the mind rambles along with the flailing limbs and the captured senses with the result that the human constitution, governed by excess, deceives the observer. Only the knowing seeker employing the powers of discrimination penetrates this illusion to the center, to Being.

Chapter 3 – Wrestling With Parmenides

B EFORE WE WRESTLE with Parmenides on the issues
of being and reality and the One and the Two (or Many),
we might sit quietly with Emerson for a moment (or
two), contemplating human experience. The goddess of the fragments tells us that human beings are two-headed, entangled in a
world of duality, and consequently deceived about the nature of
being and reality. We live in a constant state of illusion, catching
mere glimpses of reality, if we're lucky. At the outset in "Experience," an essay about both these topics, Emerson asks, "Where
do we find ourselves?" His answer is to place us on a stair, forget-
ful of our setting out and uncertain of our destination. We are,
in this life, always *en passage*.

The set of stairs establishes a trope of ascent and descent, images familiar to us. What is the nature of human "progress?" Are
we ascending or descending? Is evolution a progression to some
higher state? Is human consciousness a cause or a result? Is civi-
lization a progression or a decline in human capacity and fulfil-
ment? What is the nature and meaning of history?

Sitting quietly on the stair with us, Emerson says, "Life is not
dialectics" and "The mid-world is best." His is practical advice,
reminding us that life is made up of power and form, not thought,
and that we had best keep to the track. He says:

Life has no memory. That which proceeds in succession might be remembered, but that which is coexistent, or ejaculated from a deeper cause, as yet far from being conscious, knows not its own tendency. So it is with us, now skeptical, or without unity, because immersed in forms and effects all seeming to be of equal yet hostile value, and now religious, whilst in the reception of spiritual law....Underneath the inharmonious and trivial particulars, is a musical perfection, the Ideal always journeying with us, the heaven without rent or seam.

It is also not necessary to take this Idealism on faith. Emerson's conviction is an observation based on experience and an example of formal logic. The region where Parmenides takes us in his poem supplies signs of itself in moments of reflection and in short bursts of understanding. In fact, as Emerson concludes, "The consciousness in each man is a sliding scale, which identifies him now with the First Cause, and now with the flesh of his body; life above life, in infinite degrees." We shall return in due course to this "sliding scale," but for now it is an assurance of where we are on this set of stairs on which we find ourselves, reflecting on being and reality, somewhere in mid-world, or worlds.

"Life is not dialectics," Emerson said. It is, rather, sturdy, a matter of getting on with it. But the examined life, looking on with a reflective awareness, does imply a dialectic approach. Plato's dialectic was based on this vision of the journey of existence. In the allegory of the cave, the confined human being is finally released from bondage by the power of the dialectic and his own nature. Emerging into the sun, the reflected light of reality, the seeker, as Plato puts it, "has the power to release and leads what is best in the soul up to the contemplation of what is best in the things that are..." In other words, to being.[15]

The difference between the poem of Parmenides and the "Parmenides" of Plato is the difference between revelation and dialectic, or, if you will, myth and science. Neither is lived experience, but both seek to advance our understanding of what lies behind that experience. Plato used dialogue to expose through close examination the vital meaning of words. The "Parmenides" in particular subjects the word 'being' to such an examination. Through the dialectic exposure of four hypotheses Plato expands our understanding of the One and the Many in order to define our limits of understanding of their relationship to being. It is a paradox, and most commentators simply give up on it.

Plato's "Parmenides" is seldom taught because it appears to contradict itself at every turn and leaves the student disoriented in a textual house of mirrors. Here for example are Edith Hamilton's comments on the material: "The ordinary person will be hard put to it to discover any meaning at all. The argument runs on and on in words that appear to make sense and yet convey nothing to the mind."[16] So what is the point? Was this dialogue meant to confuse, to confound the "ordinary person?" Hardly. It is, like all of Platonic texts, an exercise.

The "Parmenides" is all about the One and the Two, or the Many, and it proceeds logically to arrive at a profound sense of *logoi*, the fundamental use and meaning of words as they attempt to describe reality. The results, as always, are partial, or suggestive, and Plato uses the figure of Parmenides to convey the essential difficulty of trying to describe the One and the indefinite Two. As we look into this matter, we will look not only at the "Parmenides," but also at "The Republic," the "Philebus," "Phaedo," and the famous Seventh Letter.

First, however, to set the scene. Parmenides and his pupil Zeno have come to Athens to celebrate the Panathenaia, the quadrennial observance of the Goddess Athena's dominion over the city of Athens. Socrates, a young man of twenty years, hears that Parmenides and Zeno have arrived in the city and he and his friends seek them out in order to hear Zeno's defense of Parmenides and to question the aging philosopher, if, that is, he will be engaged in conversation.

After listening to Zeno's "book," Socrates poses the problem to Parmenides as follows: "You assert, in your poem, that the all is One, and for this you advance admirable proofs...You assert unity; he [Zeno] no plurality; each expresses himself in such as way that your arguments seem to have nothing in common, though really they come to very much the same thing."[17] This penetrating observation from the young Socrates impresses Parmenides, who is then drawn into the discussion.

The intellectual issue in the following discussion turns on the question of whether or not there exists a unity separate and distinct from plurality (the Many) or if the One and the Many are somehow the same thing, differing only in the way in which human beings perceive or understand multiplicity. The issue is advanced through three main propositions, each in turn seeming to contradict the one before it. The crucial question at hand is, Is there a One, and if so, what is its nature?

Before we engage this discussion in earnest, however, we need to look at Plato's dialectical procedure, his entire corpus. When Whitehead said that all philosophy was nothing but footnotes to Plato, he was referring to the body of work left by the "public" Plato. It was assumed for many years that the writings of Plato represented the primary work of the Academy, that conversation was the basis of analysis and that penetrating dialectic was the tool of investigation. That something else entirely might have been going on behind closed doors was never considered, at least not until the *Seventh Letter* was discovered and analyzed.

In the famous *Seventh Letter*, Plato made the remarkable statement concerning the real work of the Academy, saying, "I certainly have composed no work in regard to it, nor shall I ever do so in the future, for there is no way of putting it in words like other studies."[18] This confession, as it were, that the dialogues do not represent or express in writing the esoteric (or covert) teaching of the Academy has left us wondering what actually did take place on a daily basis during the more than fifty years of Plato's tenure there. It is as if we might learn almost by accident that the real work in the world's universities does not in fact take place in lecture halls and laboratories, but rather that somewhere in basements and secret gatherings, adepts expose disciples to esoteric knowledge that never sees the light of day.

It is doubtful, however, that the real work of the Academy was that secretive, at least not in the way we think, for example, of the Eleusinian Mysteries. If it was, we would never have seen a verse from Theopompus, a comic playwright and contemporary of Aristophanes, who had one of his characters exclaim:

> *For one is not one at all.*
> *And Two? The two can hardly be one as*
> *Plato says.*

We can only surmise from the evidence of Aristotle and other students that much of the work was indeed mathematical, an *algebra of being* in the search of the nature of the forms and being itself. Therefore, if we want to know the nature of the One in relation to the Two, we have to think mathematically. For example, the question arises whether Two was created by increasing quantitatively from the One or from halving the One into two parts. Was the universe created by augmentation or division? This question is debated in the *Phaedo*, without explicit conclusion. The answer to that question, as we shall see below, is that both are true.

Thinking indirectly, therefore, we can look at the *Parmenides* in a new way, kind of sideways or at a slanted angle of vision. Socrates wants to know from Parmenides the true nature of the One. Parmenides sighs and prepares himself for the arduous task of explanation, knowing full well that he will not "explain" the nature of the One satisfactorily. Mere words will not serve the purpose. But words have to learn how to serve even the most esoteric purposes.

The first proposition goes like this: the One cannot have parts or be called a "whole" because to be characterized as "whole" implies parts. Also, the One cannot have a beginning or an end or any limits whatsoever. It has no shape – is neither straight nor round – and is not even a sphere. It has no place, nor can it "be" anywhere. Nor does it move in the sense of suffering alteration. It is neither at rest nor in motion, nor can it be other than or the same as itself or another. It does not occupy time. Therefore, the One in no sense exists in ways we understand that word nor can it have a name or even be discussed. How, then, do we talk about it?

The second proposition begins with the premise that any idea of the One that "is" (if that is possible) must nevertheless be thought of as a whole and therefore made of parts. But each part will be a whole unto itself and have unity and being. If One "is," there must then be number and imply the Many within it. If then the One is a plurality, unity itself is distributed by being and is necessarily Many. As a result, the One will then have a presence, which implies a shape, meaning that it must be at rest and similarly in motion. It is in the others (the Many), having contact, with itself and others, touching and not touching. It is becoming older than itself and younger both than itself and others. Finally, the One is, is becoming, is older and younger than itself, than others, and to the contrary, neither is nor is becoming. Is it, then, becoming?

Having created syntactical chaos to this point, Plato (speaking for Parmenides) entertains a third proposition. Since the One cannot both be and not be, cannot be at rest and in motion, there must be some state of transition in which its condition changes. This so-called 'change' or alteration, must take place in the instant (timelessly), present in a gap between one condition and another. The Many cannot be the One, and yet they partake of the One. The Many must be whole, having parts, thus each part has a unity, or shares in unity [suggestive of a hologram, for example]. The Many has limits but is also unlimited by virtue of its relation to the One. The One, however, cannot really have parts or else it would not be the One. It is both all things and not all things. If the One is not, or nothing, what will follow concerning it? This "It" cannot have any character whatsoever or any relation to the Many, and if there is no One, neither can there be Many. To conclude (and not), whether there is a One or not, both the One and the Many either *are* and *are not* and therefore they *appear to be* and *not appear to be* with respect to themselves. Is the One, then, a paradox?

The confusion, almost comic in its presentation, at one level is a slap at the Sophists, whose predatory practices have a similar feel about them. Court cases in Athens were often won by obfuscation of this kind. If a case cannot be understood it gets thrown out. But behind the seeming absurdity lies a truth: words cannot express the nature of the One in relation to the Many. The syntax is reminiscent of today's description of quantum mechanics and efforts to articulate the position and mass of particles. If we find one, we cannot find the other, and vice versa. One is reminded of Schrodinger's cat, which is either alive or dead depending on whether or not it is observed. Is the One a particle and a wave simultaneously?

In the original poem, the complete version of which Plato must have possessed, Being is described and not described. It has limits within lawfulness but not limits we comprehend. It is shaped like a sphere but isn't a sphere. The only definitive statement about it is that It is! And if it is, then the Many is as well and emanates from it as source. Some six hundred years later, Plotinus would seek to unravel this paradox by describing the nature of emanation from the source of being. His hierarchal explanations describe a well ordered universe, perhaps too well ordered, too obviously rational at least in terms of the language used to describe it. One wonders how Plotinus would have greeted quantum mechanics (perhaps much the way Einstein did).

Parmenides, on the other hand, was wise enough to leave the concept of being in its paradoxical state, at least in terms of any process of emanation resulting in plurality. As we have already seen, the fragments present a truth about being and a good deal of opinion (*doxa*) about everything else, opinion that human beings find attractive, comforting, and comprehensible. The truth about being and its relation to the Many is less clear and less amenable to apt description. Sense impressions simply do not yield the truth of reality, our modern instruments notwithstanding. The closer we get to isolating the smallest particles of matter/energy, the further we drift from being, at least in terms of understanding the unity of the macrocosm. And the more expansive our visual and radio telescopes, the further we get from the nature of the microcosm. The truth lies in between, in the gap, which Plato describes in the Greek as the *metaxy*. The irony is that the human being (in terms of mass) might well be the mid-point between the extremes of the macro and micro-cosmic worlds, making the mind the instrument of the gap.

In the "Philebus," Plato describes a gift from the gods, from Prometheus in fact, in the form of a saying, which is that all things (*ta panta*) that are ever said to exist, consist of a one and a many, and have in their nature a conjunction of limit and unlimitedness.[19] The so-called "conjunction" comes to us in intermediate forms between the one and its unlimited numbers. Socrates goes on to say that "...modern man, while making his one – or his many, as the case may be – more quickly or more slowly than is proper, when he has got his one proceeds to his unlimited number straightaway, allowing the intermediates to escape him."[20] Confusing though this may seem, his idea is that human tendency is to grasp on to sensual connections too quickly, seeing this as like that, but missing the larger picture through impatience. It takes a steady, patient mind to perceive the whole.

In other words, for human beings, all perceptions are relative and none are absolute, because the Absolute lies in the *metaxy*, that in-between state where human and divine perception coincide and are said to find their commonality. The faculty of perception for Plato that perceives the forms (*eidos*), and which is the same as 'essence' in Aristotle, is the soul (*psyche*) and is the source of knowing (*gnosis*). And we are reminded once again that this knowing is not an empirical process but rather is noetic. It is a spiritual insight, which is its own evidence, not requiring external proofs. And yet, if we insist on finding an empirical solution to the problem of being, our best chance is still through mathematics and in particular through the science of sacred geometry. Geometry is the science of form and substance. Mathematics is the science of essences.

The Golden Mean Proportion

If the idea of the One and the Two, or Many, seems too abstract expressed in words, then it comes to earth as mathematics and geometry in the Golden Mean Proportion. Seen by some as merely an aesthetic consideration – a pleasing configuration -- the Golden Mean Proportion is not only much more, it is also fundamental to being and to the formation of the manifest world as we perceive it.

The concept begins with the point, the One. A second point, connected to the first, either straight or curved, in space/time, constitutes a line, Two. Once having generated the line, or the Two, we cannot seem to return to the One (unity) again. Once we have the Two, the rest follow and the result is All Things (*ta panta*). A return to the One seems impossible. Once conscious, in other words, we cannot seem to return to unity. As Emerson put it, it is a terrible thing to discover that we exist. We are fragmented and seem to be forever so.

If we take this line, this Two that we have created, we can through the Golden Mean Proportion find our way back again to the point. We can divide the line at a unique point where we create a uniquely reciprocal relationship between two unequal parts of a whole, in which the small part stands in the same proportion to the large part as the large part stands to the whole. To describe the golden section geometrically, we construct a line that is one unit long. Then we divide the line into two unequal segments, such that the shorter one equals x, the longer one equals (1-x) and the ratio of the shorter segment to the longer one equals the ratio of the longer segment to the overall line; that is, $x/(1 - x) = (1 -$

x)/1. That equality leads to a quadratic equation that can be used to solve for *x*, and substituting that value back into the equality yields a common ratio of approximately 0.618.....(to infinity)

The number, 0.618...and so on to infinity, is irrational, that is, like root 2 or 5, where the numerical value cannot be resolved. Or to put it another way, its length cannot be expressed as a finite number. To the Greeks, this irrationality at the heart of perfect geometrical forms was a mystery, and indeed it remains so. The Golden Mean Rectangle, which is constructed from a Square Root of Five triangle, has about it a distinctive feature. The artist and writer Astrid Fitzgerald expressed the distinction this way:

> The Golden Mean rectangle may be increased or decreased by the addition of a square, which is symbolic in sacred geometry of the creation. This increase or decrease does not affect the proportion (the essence or inherent law). In other words, 'the remainder is perfect.'

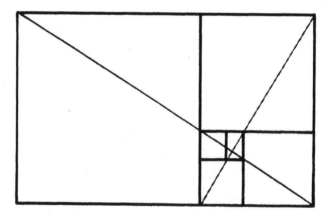

Fig. 2: Golden Mean rectangle increased by addition of squares

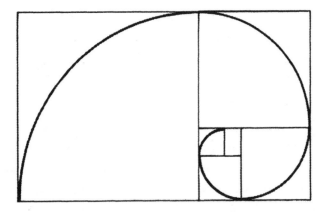

Fig. 3: Golden Mean rectangle with spiral construction

By adding an arc within each square, the formation of the Golden Mean spiral emerges. The outward spiral symbolizes expansion, creation, and the harmonic unfolding of the implicit order. The inward spiral shows the way back to the source, the still point where there are no ripples, where the phenomenal world ceases to exist, which the mystics describe as union with Brahman.[21]

The significance of this construct is two-fold. On the one hand, we see a symbolic and descriptive expression of symmetrical generation and on the other a symbolic and descriptive expression of regeneration, that is a return to the One from the Many. The spiral works both ways. Add a square and we have another golden rectangle. Subtract a square and we have another. One into Many, Many into One.

The idea of the Many can also be expressed by the third point, as discussed earlier in a consideration of Pythagoras. The function of the third point – either a triangle or circular construct was expressed in a conversation between Richard Temple and Keith Crtichlow in the 1981 *Parabola Magazine* issue devoted to the Golden Mean.

RT: I have been trying to understand how, in its absolute essence, the Golden Mean is the Trinity, the division of unity within itself into two and expressed in completion as three, yet ever remaining unity.

KC: It is true: the basic idea of a 'mean,' just the concept of a 'mean,' upon which Aristotle built the whole of his theory of the soul's perception, was that it is a particular point of balance between two extremes and therefore it has to be trinitarian. You have to have two extremes for there to be a mean, but the mean unifies those two and, as you were saying, the whole point about the Trinity is the quality of threeness which is in itself a single thing. Threeness is a single thing; 'three' is three separate things.

RT: We learn that the origin of number, like the Absolute in the Universe, is One: Unity. Creation is two: Unity dividing itself, going outwards from itself. And three, the Trinity, is the completion of the process that initiates a motion sending God out into ultimately the very last part of the universe. The Trinity exists everywhere in the universe. The fact that we can find the Golden Proportion in plants and in the structure of man shows that this law is everywhere. I came across a definition of the Golden Mean which states that it is the unity that includes both what is perceived as well as the perceiver. There are two ways [and the Golden Proportion is the only number for which this is true] mathematically, by which you can place the Golden Mean between those two points. The lesser in relation to the greater in the Golden Mean can signify that the outer is the greater and the inner is the lesser, or it can signify that the inner is the greater and the outer is the lesser. But the 'mean' is a fluctuation in between those two things. So the Yin and the Yang are as the proportions of the Golden mean unto each other, and thus chase each other dynamically in asymmetrical equilibrium.

What the Golden Mean Proportion establishes is a relationship between One (a point) and Two (a line) in such a way as to allow a return to the One from the Many expressed as a spiral continuum rather than as a conceptual leap or radical disjuncture of nature. Unlike Temple and Critchlow (among many others) those philosophers and theologians caught in dualistic structures of this/that, cannot unbend to the notion that Being is a continuous state of the articulated One, unless, of course, they conceive of that One in Pantheistic terms.

What Parmenides wanted to accomplish was a vision of the purity of Being without separating it from plurality, thus creating a fixed duality. His vision gained support from Orphic believers, whose mythology included within the human being a spark of divinity or soul emanating from the dismembered and then re-membered persona of Dionysus. The Golden Mean Proportion expresses the same dynamic and is probably why the proportion appears in Egyptian and Greek temples where the emphasis was on re-uniting the human being with his or her god.

If we look for a moment once more at the aesthetic question, we can apply the same criteria. The Golden Mean Proportion expresses the fundamental laws of generation and regeneration: the return to unity, the presence of being and its relation to the Many, the vision of unity in all things. Its beauty is an expression of those relations, indeed arises from it. In the structure of the sunflower, for example, the golden mean spiral (as it is manifest in Fibonacci numbering) appears in the formation of the seeds at the center of the flower. The One is expressed as the single seed from which the next flower will be generated (the Many).

The presence of the Golden Mean in architecture and painting and even music is beautiful because it expresses pure articulated being. We admire the beauty of the perfect circle, the square and the equilateral triangle, but the golden mean rectangle has about it a certain asymmetrical transcendence because that is exactly how it is formed. The *phi* proportion, the irrational 0.618.... is more beautiful still because it surprises us. Its elegant curve, seen so often in the formation of leaves and flowers, in shells and starfish, and even in the proportions of the human body, leads us away from rigid patterns and returns us to the unity from which we evolved.

I have presented the Golden Mean Proportion in these pages as an illustration of a principle at work in the cosmos, in art, and as a specific esoteric interest of Plato's in the "Timaeus." Since the proportion was used in temple design, particularly the Parthenon, the Academy must have included its study, especially since gaining admission to the Academy required a prior knowledge of geometry. On the exoteric level, we know, for example that Plato's philosophy of the cosmos consisted of the interaction of three essential forces: *Eros, Thanatos,* and *Dike* (the forces of passion, death and justice.)[22] These forces correspond to what we might see as creation, entropy, and harmony, or more scientifically, the conservation of energy in whole systems. The Golden Mean is the symbolic representation of regeneration within the dynamic of those three forces. As such it is the force which counteracts entropy and is the cosmic symbol of regeneration.

Plato's interest in the mathematics of being changed over the years from an expression of ideas (like the three forces) to the existence of Ideas, that is, where ideas became substantial Forms (*eidos*) existing somewhere between Being as an entity and being as an equivalent of 'cosmos.' This transformation of being into Idea wasn't really necessary, finally, and Plato's concern with the Ideas has been a distraction ever since.

Having implied that Plato created a system based on the Ideas, then we can also say that his pupil Aristotle developed his own system to challenge it. In fact, however, too much has been made of Aristotle's systematic dismantling of the Ideas and not enough of his own vision of Being based on sense experience, or realism in philosophy. Our concern, however, is with Aristotle's reaction to Parmenides.

Aristotle

Aristotle was, in a curious oxymoron, a reductive visionary. He took Plato's *Eros*, for example, one of the three great forces of the cosmos and the soul's path to the Infinite, and made it an "interest," a curiosity to know. Seeking the truth was a "delight" to him, an excellent exercise for the mind. He inherited from his teacher a passionate desire to uncover the secrets of the cosmos, but then made it an aristocratic past-time, an exploration of the things of the world. Whereas Socrates died for the truth, and Plato gave his life to it, Aristotle was a curious intellectual, the perfect university professor in the laboratory of experience, and as a result, we can say that all universities are Aristotelian. He wanted to know, but his was the curiosity of the detached, purely professional investigator, and like many "progressive" thinkers, he was too quick to dismiss the ideas of earlier seekers as obsolete, although it must be said that he respected Parmenides more than most. We begin with the "Metaphysics," the title of which is an editorial comment and not originally Aristotle's. It was, in his mind, speculation on First Causes. In reference to Parmenides, Aristotle said,

> *Of those who said the universe was one, then none succeeded in discovering a cause of this sort, except perhaps Parmenides, and he only inasmuch as he supposes that there is not only one but also in some sense two causes.*[23]

The misreading in this case (unless we are missing material Aristotle was using or the complete poem of Parmenides) comes as a result of ignoring the words of the goddess when she tells the youth, "Now I cease my truthful words concerning well-rounded truth, and *from this point on*, you must learn the opinions of the mortal world by listening to the deceptive order of my words...." Following this warning come all the references to duality and multiple causes. What Aristotle seems to interpret in the text is multiple causes where multiple opinions of causes are meant. The goddess, who symbolizes the Way of Truth, separates Truth from Opinion (*doxa*), making sure in the process that the "knowing man" understands where human inquiry has gone astray. Although Aristotle himself understands the error of multiple causes, he appears to attribute the error to Parmenides.

Next, reflecting his own bias against the views of the past, Aristotle warns his readers that the early thinkers are obsolete.

Now these thinkers, as we said, must be neglected for the purposes of the present inquiry — two of them entirely, as being a little too naive, viz. Xenophanes and Melissus; but Parmenides seems in places to speak with more insight. For, claiming that, besides the existent, nothing non-existent exists, he thinks that of necessity one thing exists, viz. the existent and nothing else (on this we have spoken more clearly in our work on nature), but being forced to follow the observed facts, and supposing the existence of that which is one in definition, but more than one according to our sensations, he now posits two causes and two principles, calling them hot and cold, i.e. fire and earth; and of these he ranges the hot with the existent, and the other with the non-existent.[24]

Here, Aristotle supposes that when Parmenides speaks in his poem of "mortal opinions," that he is referring to "being forced to follow the observed facts" and judging "according to our sensations." The result, he supposes, is that Parmenides has contra-dicted himself, whereas the poem clearly states that these are the false opinions of mortals in regard to being. That they are in some sense "natural" is nonetheless a matter of human limita-tion and should not be attributed to Parmenides' views of reality. Again, the misreading emerges from a pre-conceived rejection of earlier thinkers and is typical of Aristotle's description of the Presocratics in general.

In another instance, Aristotle reads Parmenides correctly when he says that all things are One and that this One is identi-cal with Being, but then he goes on to reject Plato on the grounds that "number cannot be a substance." Parmenides, of course, nev-er mentions the Pythagorean notion of number as substance, but Aristotle has assumed that Parmenides is Pythagorean in this regard and is using One not as a symbol of unity but as the Num-ber One as a conceptual entity in relation to subsequent num-bers. One, in this case, refers to unity and not to a substantial One as conceived by Pythagoras and expressed in the signs and symbols of geometry, except as a symbolic representation of be-ing as distinct from the Many. This misreading goes rather to Plato's notion of the Forms, which in turn does not follow from Parmenides.

Next, Aristotle once again dismisses Parmenides and the oth-er Eleatics on the issue of the One and the Many on the grounds of form, even though late in life, he admitted that he should have paid more attention to myth.

There are many causes which led them off into these explanations, and especially the fact that they framed the difficulty in an obsolete form. For they thought that all things that are would be one (viz. Being itself), if one did not join issue with and refute the saying of

Parmenides: 'For never will this be proved, that things that are not are.' They thought it necessary to prove that that which is not is; for only thus of that which is and something else-could the things that are be composed, if they are many.[25]

Aristotle appears here to be taking issue with Zeno when he says that "They thought it necessary to prove that 'that which is not is..,' whereas Parmenides was only concerned with establishing that Not-Being was impossible in order to deny the existence of Nothingness. It should be added that Paul Dirac, in our own time, examined the notion of nothingness and proved that, as the goddess declared, nothingness cannot be. A vacuum, Dirac said, is instant soup without visible soup, which when energy is added produces the soup from its inherent potential. So in a very real sense, Parmenides is correct; nothingness isn't.

Later thinkers – namely Democritus and the other Sophists – constructed a dualistic framework in which substance (in the form of 'atoms') could exist only within an entity called a void. They had the modern idea. Again, however, Parmenides is not the source of this dualism. His 'goddess' affirms the fullness of Being as the source of the Many. The mystery of the relation of the One to the Many comes in fragment 4:

See clearly with the mind how
Things far and near are one,
No matter how dispersed, Being
Does not separate from Being.

But Aristotle wants the connection to be manifestly clear and as a result, he must affirm the fundamental duality of the cosmos. If there exists a Being, a God, then it or he is necessarily 'other.'

In this matter he appears to want to agree with Parmenides, but he does so only by separating Being from plurality. This line of reasoning becomes the majority view into the Roman era and beyond and comes finally down to the concrete dualism of Thomas Aquinas. From there we pass into the modern era with a rejection of the other, the death of God, leaving human consciousness alone in the universe.

Plotinus

Plato was a careful man. As a philosopher dedicated to the truth of reality, he was also aware of his role as a citizen of Athens. In his philosophical explorations, he had arrived finally at a fundamental duality in the nature of the cosmos, not, one suspects, from intellectual conviction and noetic experience, but through a sound understanding of the nature of human existence. Late in his life, in the *Laws* (896e) he had resolved a crisis within his own consciousness by positing the existence of two souls, one good, the other evil.

The Athenian (Plato himself), who is walking through the countryside in Crete with a Cretan and a Spartan, declares that "...soul is the cause of good and evil, fair and foul, right and wrong – in fact all contraries, if we mean to assert it as the universal cause." He then has to resolve a difficulty. How can universal soul be the cause of evil? Of all the contraries? His answer, an inevitable one if Plato was to create the means by which human beings could function in the world, was to create two universal souls, one good, the other evil, hence a God who permits a positive demiurge or angel and a negative demiurge or devil to exist and carry out their wills.

As a much later disciple of Plato, Plotinus had to resolve this difficulty if he was to affirm the One and identify it with Unity and still be loyal to his master. One solution to the problem was to go back to Parmenides and the concept of Being. He does so by affirming the existence of Being (gleaned from Parmenides) while allowing for variant degrees of perception on the part of souls elevated into the realm of the divine presence. The relevant passage is from the Fifth Ennead, a long argument, but worth following.

> 10. *This is why Zeus, although the oldest of the gods and their sovereign, advances first towards that vision, followed by gods and demigods and such souls as are of strength to see. That Being appears before them from some unseen place and rising loftily over them pours its light upon all things, so that all gleams in its radiance; it upholds some beings, and they see; the lower are dazzled and turn away, unfit to gaze upon that sun, the trouble falling the more heavily on those most remote.*
>
> *Of those looking upon that Being and its content, and able to see, all take something but not all the same vision always: intently gazing, one sees the fount and principle of Justice, another is filled with the sight of Moral Wisdom, the original of that quality as found, sometimes at least, among men, copied by them in their degree from the divine virtue which, covering all the expanse, so to speak, of the Intellectual Realm is seen, last attainment of all, by those who have known already many splendid visions.*
>
> *The gods see, each singly and all as one. So, too, the souls; they see all There in right of being sprung, themselves, of that universe and therefore including all from beginning to end and having their existence There if only by that phase which belongs inherently to the Divine, though often too they are There entire, those of them that have not incurred separation.*
>
> *This vision Zeus takes, and it is for such of us, also, as share his love and appropriate our part in the Beauty There, the final object of all seeing, the entire beauty upon all things; for all There sheds radiance, and floods those that have found their way thither so that they too become beautiful; thus it will often happen that men climbing heights where the soil has taken a yellow*

glow will themselves appear so, borrowing colour from the place on which they move. The colour flowering on that other height we speak of is Beauty; or rather all There is light and beauty, through and through, for the beauty is no mere bloom upon the surface.

To those that do not see entire, the immediate impression is alone taken into account; but those drunken with this wine, filled with the nectar, all their soul penetrated by this beauty, cannot remain mere gazers: no longer is there a spectator outside gazing on an outside spectacle; the clear-eyed hold the vision within themselves, though, for the most part, they have no idea that it is within but look towards it as to something beyond them and see it as an object of vision caught by a direction of the will.

All that one sees as a spectacle is still external; one must bring the vision within and see no longer in that mode of separation but as we know ourselves; thus a man filled with a god – possessed by Apollo or by one of the Muses -- need no longer look outside for his vision of the divine being; it is but finding the strength to see divinity within.

Ennead V, Tractate VIII, 10.

The impact of this revelation was to establish the unity of Being as the source of consciousness, while at the same time asserting a continuum that the human soul varied from pure to corrupt in its ability to perceive the highest good. The argument also establishes that ignorance, not some pure evil is the source of what we see as evil (as opposed to suffering) in the world. This perception fell into line with the hierarchal vision of Plotinus, at the core of which was his theory of emanation. Being is full, lacking nothing, and this fullness overflows its nature into the next realm of being, and into the next, endlessly, like water into a terraced fountain. The overflowing of the nature of being creates realms of like nature but varied in appearance, the final appearance being the material cosmos.

The beauty of Plotinus is the manner in which he explores this fullness of being. His language is less dialectical than Plato's, less dependent on argument. Rather, as readers of Plotinus we are included in observations based on his noetic experience. In other words, Plotinus overflows as well, continuing the process of emanation. He lets us in to his inner life, whereas Plato keeps to himself, confining himself to the dialectic. Plotinus opens out to shared description, convincing us that, like the youth in Parmenides' poem, he has been on the Way of Truth. In this way, he follows Parmenides and offers us a more direct expansion of poetic revelation. Therefore, he was able to say in the Sixth Ennead, " Parmenides was right when he taught the identity of Being and Unity."

Friedrich Schelling and Eric Voegelin

The reason for introducing two more modern philosophers at this point in the discussion is two-fold. First, Friedrich Schelling (1775-1854) possessed an extraordinary mind, not only naturally gifted but also beautifully developed. Although he fell out of favor among the nineteenth century German Idealists in the wake of the sheer volume of Hegel's output, he remains a unique and valuable resource in any ontological exploration. Also, Schelling's insights into the Greek pantheon and specifically the ancient gods of Samothrace, bear directly on the nature of the goddess who introduces our youth to the realm of Being. Second, the work of Eric Voegelin (1901-1985) in the twentieth century develops a new language for the appreciation and relevance of the Presocratic philosophers in our own search for divine sources.

First, however, Schelling. The Greek island of Samothrace, as distinct from its more famous southern neighbor Samos, is a mountainous outcropping in the northern Aegean. Turbulent winds drive waves onto its rocky shores for most of the year, making it a challenge to find anchorage, even today. The island sits too far north to be strategic as an outpost guarding the Hellespont, but myth says that from its five thousand foot peak, Mt. Fengari, Poseidon watched, no doubt through heavy lenses, the battle to conquer Troy. The archaeological record of the island reveals an ancient sanctuary dating from at least the seventh century BCE (probably much older) devoted to the Great Gods, a fact known to Schelling as early as 1800. It has been assumed that the gods honored on Samothrace came from Thrace, to the north, were Pre-Greek, and remained non-Greek for many generations. However, certain aspects of the history and rituals involving these gods also recommends Anatolia as their source, home of the earliest Earth Mother cult.

From earliest times, the great gods of Samothrace were known as Axieros, Axiokersa, Axiokersos, and Kosmilos. The first and most important was Axieros, later identified or absorbed in Demeter worship. Later, Axiokersa was identified with Persephone (and Artemis), Axiokersos with Hades, and Kosmilos with Hermes. Their overall characterization as Kabeiroi (or Cabiri) does in fact locate these gods as Anatolian and relates Axieros to the earliest manifestation of the Earth Mother goddess, a fact supported by archeological finds in Central Turkey.

The Great Gods of Samothrace formed a chthonic cult with mysterious initiatory rites shrouded in secrecy. We do know that the rituals were conducted at night, that anyone might participate, and that communion with the goddess was primary. Because of Schelling's thorough knowledge of ancient languages, he was able to make a valuable connection between these nocturnal rites and the earliest cosmological myths.

We can pass over in silence the common prefix of the first three deities as not being significant for the special nature of each. But according to the literal translation for the first name, Axieros, in the Phoenician dialect can not very well mean other than "hunger," "poverty," and in consequence "yearning," "seeking."…. The raw material of this narrative is a fragment of that age-old doctrine according to which Eros is the first of the gods to proceed out of the world-egg, whereas before it there is only the night bearing the egg. For it was the teaching of all peoples who counted time by nights that the night is the most primordial of things in all of nature....But what is the essence of night , if not lack, need, and longing?[26]

In connecting the figure of Axieros to the earliest myths of creation and referring to the world-egg out of which *Eros* comes as the first god, Schelling reminds us of the isolated fragment 13 from Parmenides making the same reference to this myth: *First of all the gods she fashioned Eros.* The youth in the poem emerges from the dark night of the soul to encounter the goddess, for whom he yearns, and who in turn is anxious to impart light and wisdom to him. The mythic patterns of the poem may well reflect a ritual similar to, or even connected to, the Mysteries of Samothrace.

The youth and the goddess are possessed by longing, he to seek, she to be sought after. *Eros* is the medium of the exchange from emptiness to fullness, and it is important to emphasize the nature of *Eros* here. The force of the passion to commune goes both ways. The gods, too, yearn for human contact, and as a result, they come half way to those who yearn to be *en theos*, or "with the god." The desire for union is felt both emotionally and intellectually. In the case of Samothrace, for example, at the entrance to the inner sanctum (adyton) of the temple stood a statue of an aroused Hermes, longing after the figure of Persephone within. These themes incorporated what Nietzsche would develop as the Apollonian and Dionysian impulses in human nature and which Jung and the archetypal psychologists to follow have integrated into their theories of the human psyche.

The difficulty with psychological approaches has been the tendency to interiorize the search for divine transcendence to the point of making the individual human instrument the sole theater for this cosmic drama. Modernity has accepted the demise of the gods and substituted instead the despair of human loneliness as our prevailing condition, with the result that the ground of our being has shrunk to the dimensions of a grave. The image is Beckett's: woman gives birth squatting astride the grave and we are given a tick of time for our fall into nothingness.

In answer to this despair, religion continues to maintain a discreet distance from the divine nature as a matter of dogmatic convenience, while permitting a measured communion with officially sanctioned mystical experience. In this arid climate God maintains an otherness in the great silence of the cosmos, and the ancient sites of sacredness throughout the world offer little but nostalgia and trinkets for the curious.

Schelling wrestled with these problems all of his life, seeking to resolve the questions of the One and the Many, the Subjective and Objective, even as materialism swept into Europe in the wake of the Enlightenment. He approached the problem with this conviction: "The highest consummation of natural science would be the complete spiritualizing of all natural laws into laws of intuition and thought."[27] It is a consummation devoutly to be wished. From that premise, Schelling fought the tendencies of duality in science and philosophy through the medium of Romantic Imagination raised to the level of a transcendent philosophy. We should look to it.

Whereas Hegel overwhelmed Schelling by imposing his elaborate system of intellectual transcendence, the result was, once again, to isolate the individual mind and make it the universe of knowing. Hegel wished to discover the divine through the scientific method by employing the genius of his own (private) mind as the instrument. Schelling, on the other hand, understood the trap into which Hegel had fallen. The divine will not be known by the cursive mind, or even through scientific inquiry, but only through the grace of an intuitive insight. In fact, Schelling claimed that not even the existence of the "I" could be proven by the scientific method. Even today, science does not know what the "I" is. Parmenides would say, "Is" and leave the "I" to defend itself.

In Parmenides, we see the same grace at work. The goddess is presented as a transcendent force showering the seeker with wisdom. Parmenides himself makes no claim to have arrived at his knowledge by himself, or through his own efforts. The nature of Being is not presented as a work of the reason, but rather as a surprising gift, an experience without precedent and without even a hint of prior knowledge. It literally comes out of nowhere. It is revelation. The details remain to be worked out, as Plato and later philosophers attempted.

We ask, then, who or what is the goddess? She is not an icon or an idol, nor is she merely a symbol of intuitive understanding. She is a reality, a conclusion which may beg the question as to what reality is, but that is what Parmenides would have us understand. Given the history of the feminine divine in Greece, we can say that she is a spirit of the cosmos, responding to human longing through a longing of her own, with *Eros* as the medium of contact. She is the youth's "heart's desire." As such, she is an ordering force within the soul.

The important theme of "ordering" brings us to the work of Voegelin. With his monumental five volume *Order and History*, political philosopher Eric Voegelin became in effect the twentieth century Plato, not merely in the sense of reaffirming Plato's importance (although that was a benefit) but in restoring the divine center to the movement of human history without the burdens of religious layering. The premise of his work can be found in his statement in *Israel and Revelation*, "The spirit lives in the world as an ordering force in the souls of human beings."[28]

In addition to this remark is one from an essay entitled "The Eclipse of Reality," from the Collected Works. He defines philosophy as "....the exegesis of man's existence in tension toward the divine ground."[29] Such a definition places Voegelin firmly on Platonic and Parmenidean ground.

A brief comment made by Voegelin on the work of Schelling helps to smooth the transition into the twentieth century and the crisis of modernity.

> Man cannot escape the finiteness of his particular existence. His will to perfection in life is frustrated insofar as the nature under him can never be completely spiritualized. The independent ground in him resists conquest.
> This aspect of existence is revealed experientially in the "tone" of melancholy ."The darkest and deepest in human nature is yearning (Sehnsucht), as it were the inner gravitation of the soul; hence in its deepest it is melancholy" (in German Schwerkraft and Schwermut). In this melancholy is founded the sympathy of man with nature.[30]

Both Schelling and Voegelin are concerned with "the inner gravitation of the soul" in human duality. They see it as a force of existence itself weighing us down and keeping us from the "Way of Truth." The virtue of Voegelin's work in the twentieth century was to confront this "grave" problem without succumbing to existential angst. It was no small feat.

Given the bias of the twentieth century towards materialism and its attendant religious dualism, this philosophical task has been, for the most part, ignored. Although Voegelin has a small and passionate following among contemporary historians and philosophers, he is generally regarded by the academy as an irrelevant reactionary and is not accorded a significant role in the debate. But eventually Voegelin will prove to be crucial to the philosophical enterprise going forward, if only because he keeps open the door to mystery through an empirical logic that, although highly complex, strikes at the very heart of the important questions of human existence. As I hope to demonstrate below, Voegelin's compact language deserves close attention, and his interest in Parmenides should spark renewed interest in all the Presocratic thinkers, particularly if not filtered through Plato and Aristotle first. The trouble is that for most scholars, getting back to 500 BCE without stopping at the Academy first is next to impossible.

Voegelin's interest in Parmenides begins in a long section in *The World of the Polis*, volume two, of *Order and History*. So important was Parmenides to his thesis, that Voegelin returned to him in the unfinished volume five, *In Search of Order*, where the theme of Being and the human quest for the truth of reality reaches its climax. But, first things first.

The quest for the truth begins with "the mystical transport," Voegelin's term for the mythological and symbolic means by which the "knowing man" is able to transcend the ordinary world of *doxa* and enters into dialogue with divine sources. Voegelin puts it this way:

> The process in which the soul disengages itself from collective existence and achieves attunement with transcendent-divine reality, was in both instances [Hellenic and Israelite history] on principle the same – with the important difference, however, that in no period of Jewish history before the appearance of Christ had the articulation of the life of the soul, as well as the way of the truth, reached an intenseness and a precision of symbolism comparable with the Hellenic of the fifth and fourth centuries BC.[31]

Here we begin to see how Voegelin as the writer and thinker approaches his thesis. It is a given for him that the human soul not only exists, but also that it possesses faculties and qualities making it capable of movement within the broader transcendent-divine reality. It is also given that the movement of the soul in human existence has a history of its own, a history in which the figure of Parmenides plays a major role.

The next step is to consider the nature of the "mystical transport" by which the young Parmenides enters into the realm of divine truth and learns the crucial difference between truth and opinion. Voegelin describes the mythological basis of the imagery as having derived from Hesiod and from Solon, two authorities in Hellenic order whose symbols would have been readily understood -- hence the chariot, horses, maiden guides and realm of Night guarded by the figure of Justice. Parmenides means to indicate that this "mystical transport" represents an intuitive leap of understanding by virtue of a vision by a man graced with insight. By what means he achieved this insight is left to us to discover. What Voegelin does next is to quote a passage from Plato's "Timaeus" in order to demonstrate the formulation in question. The following selection is Jowatt's translation of section 90 a-b:

And we should consider that God gave the sovereign part of the human soul to be the divinity of each one, being that part which, as we say, dwells at the top of the body, inasmuch as we are a plant not of an earthly but of a heavenly growth, raises us from earth to our kindred who are in heaven. And in this we say truly; for the divine power suspended the head and root of us from that place where the generation of the soul first began, and thus made the whole body upright. When a man is always occupied with the cravings of desire and ambition, and is eagerly striving to satisfy them, all his thoughts must be mortal, and, as far as it is possible altogether to become such, he must be mortal every whit, because he has cherished his mortal part. But he who has been earnest in the love of knowledge and of true wisdom, and has exercised his intellect more than any other part of him, must have thoughts immortal and divine, if he attain truth, and in so far as human nature is capable of sharing in immortality, he must altogether be immortal; and since he is ever cherishing the divine power, and has the divinity within him in perfect order, he will be perfectly happy. Now there is only one way of taking care of things, and this is to give to each the food and motion which are natural to it. And the motions which are naturally akin to the divine principle within us are the thoughts and revolutions of the universe. These each man should follow, and correct the courses of the head which were corrupted at our birth, and by learning the harmonies and revolutions of the universe, should assimilate the thinking being to the thought, renewing his original nature, and having assimilated them should attain to that perfect life which the gods have set before mankind, both for the present and the future.

This passage expresses the scale of being within human existence and is important for its non-dualistic framework. Hence, "The divine principle within us are the thoughts and revolutions of the universe." Voegelin is convinced that this passage is directly from the thought of Parmenides and develops what he called "a minimum dogma of the soul" in Greek thinking. He goes even further to assert that "The experience of immortality is a fundamental human experience which historically precedes the discovery of the soul as the source of such knowledge."[32] The soul participates in the divine realm if human perception is attuned to the movement towards it. Voegelin describes it this way:

The cultivation of the immortal part through occupation of the mind with things immortal and divine is understood as a

85

"cult" of the divine, symbolized as the daimon; and through a life of such cult practice the soul itself will become eudaimon [blessed].[33]

The next step after the "mystical transport" into the realm of the truth is the beginning of the "cultivation of the immortal part." This cultivation begins with contemplation on the *eon*, Being, which for Voegelin signals the beginning of philosophy. By this assertion he means that the concept of being for the first time enters into what he calls, "experiential grasp."[34] The organ doing the grasping is *Nous*, Mind, which brings into the present what is absent to the senses. *Nous* becomes the organ of cognition and is always considered by Parmenides as inferior to Being, which the mind cognizes through the *Logos*.

Voegelin's grasp of the order of being (eon) as it is cognized by *Nous* through the medium of the *Logos* is a major contribution to the study of noetic speculation, particularly when these terms are located in relation to the Way (*hodos*) . He says, "The meaning of 'way,' of the *hodos*, shifts in this opening from the mystical to the logical way, foreshadowing the meaning of methodos, of the method of scientific inquiry."[35]

Here then is the source of what we have called "formal logic" in the noetic quest, shown to us by Parmenides as a transformation of the "mystical transport" into an inquiry on the 'way' of the Mind in its quest for knowledge and understanding. The crucial matter is that the way of the mind is based on its inherent laws within individual experience and not simply on mystical teaching. The philosopher – Parmenides in this case – shows us the way that we are to proceed if the way to truth is the desire of our hearts. The transference over time from Parmenides to us is accomplished by what Voegelin refers to as "the self-contained homogeneous continuum [of] the spacial predicate of Being, corresponding to the temporal Now."

The compactness of that formulation hides (or evades) a fuller description of the continuum of being within unity. Rather than seeing Being as Other opposing the Many, Parmenides intends us to see Being (which he prefers to describe as 'Is!') in relation to the All (*pan*). Voegelin describes the relation in this way:

> This All is a "Living Being" (*zoon*), comprising all other living beings, including gods and men, within it. As a Living Being it consists of an intelligible structure, the *Nous*, formatively invested in a life force, the Psyche, which in turn is embodied in materials accessible to sense perception, in the *Soma*. The complex of *Nous*-in-Psyche-in-*Soma* symbolizes the structure of cosmic reality, regarding the comprehending All as well as its parts.[36]

Here then is the indication of how the One becomes the All through the intervention and participation of the *Nous*. The human quest for the truth of reality seeks the One from the realm of the Many. It is meditative consciousness that bridges the distance through what Plato called the *metaxy* or the space between the human and divine realms.

Human consciousness is a 'between' faculty. Voegelin puts the case in a complex formulation: "There is no truth of reality other than the reality of the truth manifesting itself in the quest."[37] He appears to be saying that once the seeking human being arrives on the Way, limited to existence, there must of necessity be a limit to our grasp of the truth of reality. In other words, for Voegelin what lies beyond existence remains a mystery to human awareness and experience, notwithstanding the testaments of the avatars and enlightened ones. The role of the philosopher in this process is to avoid the doctrinaire, or, to put it another way, to remain independent of dogmas while seeking the truth.

Therefore, although the truth of Being is the object of philosophical inquiry, that truth can only be framed in human noetic experience. The key to that statement, of course, is in the use and meaning of the word 'noetic.' As we have already said, the *Nous* was to the Greek the cognizing faculty of the human mind. As such it was a differentiating faculty, capable of perceiving distinctions between sense-based fact, human opinion and transcendent realities. It was the gifted province of Parmenides' Knowing Man. Voegelin's term for this experience was "Noetic Differentiation." In a sense the phrase replaced a word like 'revelation' because this term was later codified by religious dogma and restricted by and to hierarchal authority, rendering it useless to philosophy.

Historically, the noetic insights of the Presocratics were taken up by the various schools (the Academy, the Sophists, the Lyceum, and so on) and made the dogma of their age, which in turn provoked destructive skepticism in later ages. This pattern has always functioned in matters of discovery. In our own history, for example, the noetic insights of Ralph Waldo Emerson were dogmatized by followers into Transcendental Idealism only to be skeptically dismissed by the Realists of the early twentieth century. The point is that a level of dogmatism had to enter in before skepticism began its work. In a real sense, the original noetic insights remain intact.

What is ironic is that the more insightful the noetic experience, the more quickly a dogmatism sets in and the more strident the skeptical reaction. In the case of Parmenides, his formulation of Being sparked a revolution in philosophical thought, starting with his pupil Zeno and spreading quickly to Athens, where Socrates, Anaxagoras, Plato and then Aristotle took up the case. It was Aristotle, of course, who finally rejected the original insights as being inconsistent with his new definition of human reason. It might be said, then, that among the later thinkers, it was Aristotle who lacked the personal experience of noetic insight as a result of the exclusionary precision of his categorizing mind.

Ever since human beings began to ask the question "What is reality?" they have understood that basing an answer on what the senses report limits the possibilities. Those who are content with a sense-based definition of reality are generally content with the world they thus construct, one they can see, touch, hear, taste and smell. If they worry at all about what comes after this sense-based experience, they have the comforts of religion to ease their anxiety and smooth the way to the next world or the formless void. And when things go wrong, they blame the gods for their misery and perform various rites of expiation and pleas for mercy.

Parmenides, on the other hand, enters the presence of the gods as a 'knowing man' without fault and indeed with good fortune preceding him. He is taken by the right hand and treated with respect. The gods grant him answers to his queries and give him the means of living with happiness and understanding. Not even the heavy hand of Justice stays his progress but instead opens the gate to knowledge and understanding without delay. Justice allows him to "cross over" because it is for the best that the way of truth be known to him.

But problems remain. As Plato was to demonstrate in the allegory of the cave in book seven of "The Republic," it is those who are confined to the shadows of the sensory cave, chained to *Doxa*, who live in ignorance and suffering. Once released by the powers of *Eros* (the desire of the heart) to seek the truth, they reach the light of day and begin to experience reality. But as Plato understood, the noetic insight thus achieved, is a lonely proposition. It cannot be shared collectively because those still confined below haven't the capacity to differentiate between shadows and light. Their *Nous* remains undeveloped, rigid in sense-based perception because their own experience is confined.

In Plato's "Parmenides" we see first hand the problem of the teacher who returns from the light of day to the cave, in this case Athens. Parmenides comes to Athens to take part in the Panathenaia. He is accosted by the youthful Socrates and asked to elaborate on his noetic insights. Years have passed since his youthful experience and in the intervening time a veil of words has descended between it and others. The truth cannot be expressed other than the way it was received originally. The shift from experience to text, even spoken, renders the noetic event too distant, even irretrievable. The answer to this dilemma may very well lay hidden in the third part of the poem, in the *doxa* of human experience. If the truth of reality is to be found in the glimpse of Being afforded the seeker, then why does the goddess insist on describing in such detail the world of delusion and ignorance?

The experience of the Truth as perceived by the *Nous* must of necessity be transmitted through the *logos*, or 'account' of the goddess. She has to tell the story of Being. Human beings are in fact confined in their understanding to this *Logos*. As second-hand observers we understand nothing until we hear the story told. Voegelin describes the relation this way:

The *Nous* is discovered as the organ of cognition that will bring consensual, intelligible reality into the grasp of man. At this point, however, some caution is necessary; for the *Nous* is a rather compact symbol, and even in Aristotle it still has an amplitude of meaning from intellection to faith. In order not to read later, more differentiated meanings into the term, we should understand it strictly as the organ of the soul that brings "Being" into grasp, so that its further determination will depend on the meaning of "Being." Moreover, the *Nous*, while it brings Being into grasp, does not articulate its content. The content of Being is articulated by a further faculty that appears on this occasion for the first time, by the *logos* in the narrower sense of logical argument.[38]

It is this function of this narrow *logos* as "logical argument" that allows the nature of Being to be transmitted across experiential boundaries to the seeking mind, from Parmenides to us through the medium of the *logos*. What is important is the relation between Being, *Nous* and *logos* in the hierarchy of human perception.

Nous must always remain subservient to and yet associated with Being. In turn, the *logos* remains subservient to *nous*. The mythological hierarchy of the Greeks expressed this hierarchy in the figure of Zeus as *Nous* and his son Apollo as *Logos*. It was this connection that allowed Paul of Tarsus to appear years later in Athens and to speak of the *Logos* as Jesus the Son of God. The Greeks understood this connection clearly, just as they were able to see the feminine aspect of Wisdom embodied in Athena. To this day, Greek Christianity is held together by this association with the *Logos*, both inherent in Paul's letters and the Gospel of John.

CHAPTER 4 – THE WAY OF TRUTH

PARMENIDES PRESENTS US with two problems, both with similar features. The first is the tension between the One and the Many, a perennial challenge since the birth of philosophy. Is the One the only reality? If so, does that make the Many an illusion, or *Maya*, according to Eastern cosmologies? Or, are the One and the Many somehow both real, yet related in some way? And does that conclusion make the term "real" meaningless? And, is the existence of Being somehow opposed to the existence of Becoming? On the latter question, as yet overtly unexamined in this text but always lurking in the background, I refer first to the wisdom of Sri Aurobindo, surely one of the great ecumenical minds of the twentieth century. Aurobindo's philosophy bridged the East and West and is usually filed under Advaita Yoga, but only so as to distinguish him from the Vedantists and the Buddhists. In fact, Aurobindo succeeded in unifying a number of philosophic positions in his "considering wisdom," making him unique in his vision and unsurpassed in his expansiveness.

To set the stage for this discussion, I refer to a passage in Aurobindo's essay entitled "The Ascending Unity." Speaking of the universal human search for the truth of reality, Aurobindo describes the patterns of thought typical of man's reasoning:

Being and Becoming are to his clean-cutting confidently
trenchant mind two opposite categories, of which one or the
other must be denied, or made a temporary construction
or a sum, or sicklied over with the pale hue of illusion, and
not Becoming accepted as an eternal display of Being. These
conceptions of the sense-guided or the intellectual reason
still pursue us, but a considering wisdom comes more and
more to perceive that conclusive and satisfying as they may
seem and helpful though they may be for action of life, action of mind, action of spirit, they are yet, as we now put
them, constructions. There is a truth behind them, but a
truth which does not really permit of these isolations. Our
classifications set up too rigid walls; all borders are borders
only and not impassable gulfs. The one variable Spirit in
things carries over all of himself into each form of his omnipresence; the self, the Being is at once unique in each, common in our collectivities and one in all beings. God moves
in many ways at once in his own indivisible unity.[39]

This language resolves opposites and is found in the ambi-
guities of the extant fragments of Parmenides and also, one must
venture, in the gaps as well. What Aurobindo has expressed in
this passage is the substance of what the goddess tells the youth,
whose trenchant mind is filled with polar oppositions, and in fact
is how his brain is naturally structured. As human beings we perceive the world in oppositions in order to survive in it and yet we
can, with effort, know intuitively that the One overarches any
seeming dualities in its infinitude and harmonizing character.

The next passage from Aurobindo, from his essay on Heraclitus, whose insights we will discuss below, resolve the seeming
oppositions of the One and the Many, or "All Things."

All things then are in their reality and substance and law and reason of their being the One; the One in its shapes, values, changings becomes really all things. It changes and is yet immutable: for it does not increase or diminish, nor does it lose for a moment its eternal nature and identity which is that of the ever-living Fire. Many values which reduce themselves to the same standard and judge of all values; many forces which go back to the same unalterable energy; many becomings which both represent and amount to one identical Being.[40]

Although the reference to ever-living Fire is specific to Hera-clitus, that same "undiluted Fire" lives at the center of all things in Parmenides. In the human vision of reality, it is fire which as energy drives the universe, giving it the light and warmth in which we have our being. Fire as light, therefore, is an essential medium in both the One and the Many and resolves the seeming oppositions between the two.

Aurobindo paints with a broad brush, sweeping away minor contradictions in the interest of laying out his vision. As a result, he sweeps over details in his desire to aid the ordinary human mind in its preference for familiar landscapes and portraits. Such a huge canvas stuns us into an awed silence. In this, he appears an emissary from the gods as opposed to a scholar representing human disciplines. Perhaps there are other more human guides.

At our more mundane level, we are interested in finding our way on the road to truth. Our immediate guide is Parmenides and his poem. The Way of Truth described by Parmenides has as its dominant signpost the guidance of a goddess, a spiritual personification of great love and wisdom. She treats the seeker with respect and offers sound direction as well as transcendent knowledge. This model was emulated by Plato years later in his "Symposium," in which the similar figure of Diotima offers instruction and wisdom to the young Socrates. We are justified, I believe, in considering this important dialogue as an extension of the fragments of Parmenides.

It is not the purpose of this chapter to rehearse the events of the "Symposium" in any detail, except to remind the reader that this important dialogue, so clear in its structure and subject matter, affirms the central place of love in human and divine affairs. As the conversation moves from the lowest to the highest aspects of love, Socrates recounts his instruction from Diotima many years before. It is she who explains the nature of divine *Eros* and its/his role as a spirit and guide to human aspiration.

The following passage from Eric Voegelin's *The Ecumenic Age*, volume four of *Order and History*, sets the stage for this discussion:

> The truth of existence in erotic tension is conveyed by the prophetess Diotima to Socrates. The dialogue of the soul between Socrates and Diotima, reported by Socrates as his contribution to a dialogue on *Eros* that is a dialogue in Plato's soul, retold by to friends by one Apollodoros who, years ago, had heard it from Aristodemus, who, years ago, had been present at the Banquet, is the artfully circumvallated setting for the truth of the *Metaxy*. For this truth is not information about reality but the event in which the process of the truth becomes luminous to itself. It is not information received, but an insight arising from the dialogue of the soul when it "dialectically" investigates its own suspense "between knowledge and ignorance."[41]

Voegelin presses these points continuously in all of his work. First, the dialogues of Plato are dialogues within the soul of the philosopher, made explicit as the dialectic of philosophical investigation. Second, *Eros* is a spiritual force connecting divine power and presence with the human soul, with the point of connection being the *metaxy*, that gap between where the divine realm meets the human realm and where the One and Many have their interface. Third, *Eros* moves both ways, from the human soul as desire and from the divine as spiritual emanation. It is the conduit through and by which knowledge is transmitted.

In the Parmenides poem, the youth has already discovered the nature of the *metaxy* and with the desire of his heart has taken to the road of truth in order to move from ignorance to knowledge through its portal. The prophetess Diotima, on the other hand, is a mortal who has traveled that road herself and who transmits its signposts to Socrates, whom she considers worthy of the knowledge. That she is a woman is representative of the exalted feminine principle, that nurturing aspect of the soul giving birth to wisdom, which in its representations is always feminine.

She is described by Socrates as a woman of broad learning but most important as one whose prophetic powers postponed for ten years the Great Plague in Athens. Diotima explains that *Eros* is not a god but rather a spirit, one which moves in the mid-world between ignorance and knowledge, between the human and divine worlds. *Eros* is an envoy and an interpreter and the medium of the prophetic arts. *Eros* is the efficient power in sacrifice, initiation, incantation, sorcery, and divination.

Further, *Eros* is the son (spirit being a masculine force) of Plenty and Poverty, two attributes having the qualities of fullness, excess, resources, riches and knowledge, on the one hand, and emptiness, penury, starvation, and ignorance on the other. Such is his parentage that *Eros* knows both worlds and moves between them to ease the burdens of both.

Love, Diotima explains, is the seeker after elusive beauty, and she instructs the ignorant in the love of the physical, intellectual, artistic and spiritual nature of the beautiful. Human beings must move through these stages of knowledge, not stopping at one or skipping over any aspect of beauty on their way. Some, of course, never rise above the love of physical beauty, while others become beguiled by intellectual beauty or artistic beauty and never reach beyond to the realm of spiritual beauty, or the divine essence.

The sequence by and through which the human soul must pass gives us a clue to the bridge between the One and the Many. Human desire for happiness passes through the personal to the social to the philosophical to the spiritual realms. All are related and integrated into the truth of reality. Knowledge is not a matter of choosing one world over another, but is rather a gradual awareness of higher and higher aspects of beauty, the good, and finally, truth.

Next, Diotima explores with Socrates the nature of immortality, which she explains has the same aspects of movement from ignorance to knowledge. The first mature human impulse is to procreate, making sure that our seed is planted to preserve some aspect of ourselves into the next generation. This instinct, she explains, is no different from the religious faith in living on after death. Our desires reach out into the social and artistic worlds as well. The desire to live forever in the minds of others evokes the desire for undying fame, either in deed or works. Socrates achieved immortality through the manner of his death, Plato through the products of his work. It is said, in fact, that he died in the act of writing.

Diotima ends her instruction by pointing to the ultimate gift of *Eros*, a glimpse of "beauty's very self – unsullied, unalloyed, and freed from mortal taint...."[42] Finally, she describes the means by which the vision becomes what Voegelin calls "luminous to itself."

And remember, she said, that it is only when he discerns beauty itself through what makes it visible that a man will be quickened with the true, and not the seeming virtue – for it is virtue's self that quickens him, not virtue's semblance. And when he has brought forth and reared this perfect virtue, he shall be called the friend of god, and if ever it is given to man to put on immortality, it shall be given to him.[43]

Here, then, is the central image of the "Symposium." The virtue of wisdom is the child of beauty, conceived and given life in the soul by the perception of beauty in its highest state. The language of procreation in this final imagery connects the worlds of Being and *doxa* in the truth of reality. It is not that the body, with its needs and desires, stands in the way of spiritual truth. Rather, it points the way. The natural instincts within the body, mind and soul are woven together in the fabric of human life, but only when the highest instincts are given their freedom are we fulfilled.

Immortality, Diotima states, is a gift to those who bring forth and rear this perfect virtue. We become as gods. In the "Symposium," just as Socrates finishes his tale, the drunken Alkibiades staggers in and disrupts the proceedings, bringing the banquet to a chaotic end. He reminds us of the weakness of human intentions. Every time he looks at Socrates, he feels ashamed, knowing that he falls short of the master's expectations. It is Socrates who is capable of every sacrifice, and it is clear from Alkibiades' description that the master has achieved all the aspects of love spoken about by Diotima. He is no hypocrite, but has mastered the instruction given him. Alkibiades, then, is not so much the symbol of failed love as he is the arrow that points to Socrates as the master of love.

The Way of Truth is embarked upon alone, but we have guidance from that aspect of the soul which already possesses the right knowledge and memory of the way. We recognize the guidance as genuine because it always has the aspect of beauty. And in case we are confused about what constitutes beauty, we need only remember the Thomist triad of wholeness, harmony and radiance. These are the characteristics of artistic beauty as well as the fruits of spiritual insight. Wholeness is the One, harmony the perfection of the sphere, and radiance the emanation of light from Being.

Parmenides and Heraclitus

A summary conclusion, departing fully from the received tradition, suggests that Parmenides and Heraclitus, although contrasting in tone, are nonetheless of similar mind. Coming from opposite ends of the road, they arrive at the same place. First, two fragments: Parmenides 5: *It matters not at all from which point I begin/As I will return once more to the same place.* And from Heraclitus, Fragment 7: *The way up and the way down are one and the same.*

These two explorers only *appear* to begin in different places on the circle of reality. Parmenides begins with Being, using the mechanism of the "sacred transport" to elevate the seeker to the sanctuary of being, from which point the truth is known. Heraclitus, on the other hand, begins with the ordinary human perceptions of things and works his way "up" by inference and instigation into the center of being. Together, they form a powerful ontological team, working together, not in opposition. They are the Plato and Aristotle at the end of the Axial Age, differing but sharing a similar vision of reality.

In my *Remembering Heraclitus* (Lindisfarne, 2000), I described the method of Heraclitus in this way:

Knowing that human beings are caught in body-mind duality, Heraclitus first breaks down the easy oppositions of sensory perception and yet also establishes the necessity of opposing tension as the means by which the *Logos* creates and sustains the universe in unity. When he states that strife is necessary, he shows how it serves us well when we understand how the back-bending tension and release inherent in the bow, the lyre, and life itself give birth to new forms and are able to penetrate the opaque layers of habit built up by deadening sleep. (p.143)

The reader may be able to discern in this prose a different tone from the present text, a tone resulting from the sometimes stinging means employed by Heraclitus in cutting through the thick layers of perception common to a vision that begins in ordinary experience and works its way up to a higher plane. Parmenides, on the other hand, already standing there in the presence of the goddess, sings the arias of truth and beauty in elegiac tones. His revelations are more reminiscent of the Songs of David, whereas Heraclitus sounds more like the admonitions of Jeremiah. Nonetheless, and amazingly, the *logos* carries the same insights.

The Heraclitus fragments approach the realm of the divine only so far as the *metaxy*, that in-between state where the *Nous* of Being meets the *Nous* in the human instrument through the medium of the *Logos*. It is Heraclitus who elevated the *Logos* from a common word to the level of Being itself as part of his myth-destroying insights. Parmenides, being of a more compassionate nature, enveloped himself in the cloud of *Logos* and rained its nourishment on the world. We can see the contrast in character between the two philosophers in their revelatory methods.

When Heraclitus tells us that we cannot step twice in the same river, he shakes us loose from our ordinary perception of a river as object in order to introduce his notion of flux. To us, a river looks the same always, except when it swells with the spring rains or runs shallow in late summer. But by showing us that a river changes perpetually with different waters, we see the movement as the evanescent nature of ordinary reality. Our minds break free of opinion-based perceptions to prepare us for the truth of reality.

When we actually step into the river, we experience the ever-changing flow of life as it passes. We feel it at our feet, where normally the ground is still and solid. And yet, in the eternal Now, in the instant, we and the river are one as we enter the flow of space/time. Gradually, the temperature of our body seems to adjust, to become the temperature of the water. Differences disappear. Identity appears. We don't feel the separation and yet there it is, flowing in and around us, ever-changing, never the same.

Consider Heraclitus Fragment 10: *Everything taken together is whole but also not whole, what is being brought together and taken apart, what is in tune and out of tune; out of diversity there comes unity, and out of unity diversity.* Parmenides, too, helps us with this formulation, coming at the same premise from the other direction. We have in our minds the image of the sphere of Being out of which emerges diversity with the guidance of the goddess who steers all things. In moments of meditative stillness, we expand into our surroundings in spirals of awareness. Emerson had it right in "Circles" when he said, "Our life is an apprenticeship to the truth that around every circle another can be drawn; that there is no end in nature, but every end is a beginning."

Similarly, Heraclitus says much the same thing in Fragment 24: *This cosmos [the unity of all that is] was not made by immortal or mortal beings, but always was, is and will be an eternal fire, arising and subsiding in measure.* The Being of Parmenides resides both at the center and throughout this eternal, breathing cosmos of Heraclitus. It is here that the two come together, working together like the action of a bow, with a back-turning tension of opposites and yet in perfect unity to let truth fly outward.

Finally, *Nous* grasps the whole without being the whole because it interpenetrates the sphere of Being and the human intellect. Heraclitus' Fragment 34 makes the point: *To be wise is one thing: to know the thought that directs all things through all things.* The *Nous* of Being, which Heraclitus says both consents and does not consent to be called Zeus, Bright Consciousness, is the means through which Being orders the cosmos.

The poem of Parmenides and the prose fragments of Heraclitus are sufficient for any age and any alert seeker of knowledge. They are lessons going back to the origins of speculative philosophy as an answer to a timeless dilemma. What Parmenides in particular accomplished was monumental, seen from any distance, but most important seen purely and not through the filters of later philosophy. He articulated the centrality of Being and brought it into the world without denying the world. With a little later help from Plato, whose dialogue filled in the gaps in the loss of the whole of Parmenides, we were given the keys to understanding. Plato adds the Good to lead to the truth of reality. We need only follow the signs.

Being is. We are in it as opposed to it being in us. And yet it pervades us by its very nature as emanation. We can know Being by waking to its presence and by expanding into its presence and never contracting so as to lose contact with it. The contracted self knows nothing, sees nothing, understands nothing. As Heraclitus said, it is the curse of a private (separated) understanding. It is the small ego living separately. The Being of Parmenides is larger than the world and the universe, even as the latter expands and increasingly defies adequate description. Being is beyond space/time and yet orders space/time. It is uncreated and unmoving. From its essence all that is, is.

Love of the truth is the means by which human consciousness comes to know Being. Love does not "exist." It is. Anyone who has loved knows this. Love is experienced as an opening out of the heart into the circles of experience, combined with an overwhelming desire to know fully the beloved. Love is not mere curiosity, which is the emotional equivalent of personal ambition, nor is it satisfied with mere ideas and formulations. Love also possesses discrimination, which is a function of the heart working together with the intellect. This integration of heart and discriminating mind prevents us from mistaking opinion for truth. As such it is not skepticism, which lacks trust, but is rather a silent waiting upon the truth until it is joyfully recognized.

Beauty is an essential quality of the truth and is the greatest challenge to the discrimination. What we call good taste in matters of beauty is a superficial indication of an awareness of universal value. What we call "good taste" begins as sensory discrimination and involves all the senses working together with a discerning mind. Its major attribute is an integration of qualities into a harmonious whole, an overall impression of beauty that points to Being without describing it but which opens the heart physically, emotionally and spiritually. We are given suggestions of this opening out in moments of collective devotion, glimpses of universal understanding, and exposure to sublime art.

No doubt Parmenides sang his poem to a community of seekers. It was said that he was a commanding presence. He no doubt possessed a fine voice, musical training, and that projected a sense of beauty and good taste. The flowing hexameters of his verse made a harmonious whole and the *logos*/vision no doubt moved his listeners and opened their hearts to its depths. There on the western coast of Italy, with the sun sinking into the sea, with the columns of a temple dedicated to the goddess rising against the evening sky, the poet sang.

A modern expression of the moment is Wallace Steven's "Of Mere Being."

> The palm at the end of the mind,
> Beyond the last thought, rises
> In the bronze decor,
>
> A gold-feathered bird
> Sings in the palm, without human meaning,
> Without human feeling, a foreign song.
>
> You know then that it is not the reason
> That makes us happy or unhappy.
> The bird sings. Its feathers shine.
>
> The palm stands on the edge of space.
> The wind moves slowly in the branches.
> The bird's fire-fangled feathers dangle down.

We come closest to such beauty in our culture, perhaps, when we hear great music out in nature or in a great cathedral, together with other seekers of beauty. But so closed down are our spiritual senses most of the time that these moments are often overwhelming and our natural powers of discrimination are swept away by waves of sentimental feeling, and the moment is lost. Or perhaps the music is too familiar and we cannot approach it with an original presence.

Encountering genuine beauty is difficult in our time. The experience of it comes unbidden, by surprise, when we least expect to find it. Anticipation dampens this encounter because the ego rises up to guard itself from an experience which might threaten its autonomy and its control over what it thinks is reality. The ordinary human experience is such that we settle for a contracted world, a comfortable set of circumstances, and a picture of reality that we think we can control by ourselves. In such circumstances a false sense of judgement filters out impressions which might lift us out of our comfort zone into a transcendent space.

As a result, we are often content with the more comforting beauties of nature. What we think of as the beauty of nature may suffice, but it takes a special eye to see beyond the random expression of trees and scudding clouds into the core, where, as Heraclitus told us, nature loves to hide. The soaring mountains, a hidden waterfall, the sweep of a broad valley suddenly encountered, these feed the starving soul and may prepare the way, but they are not in themselves a sufficient emblem of Being, whose harmonies are more severe by comparison.

A true integration of the human senses into the expanded attributes of mind, heart and soul places the seer in relation to the scenery in such a way that the observer becomes what is observed, but then, our destiny as human beings is to report what we are allowed to see, framing in the work of our hands the life-enhancing desires of our hearts and the perceptions of our minds. Only the fullest integration of these faculties reveals the truth of reality. Anything less is sentimentality, which is either an excess of feeling or a partial glimpse of beauty, a mere seductive slice of the truth.

Again, it is the ego (or 'small' self) that reduces the potential to what it thinks of as manageable terms. The ego manifests its presence in personal attitudes that go on display when we confront the world on a daily basis. The ego at different times exhibits fear, hesitation, bravado, skepticism, anger, withdrawal, lust, depression, anxiety, to name a few of its games we meet every day. Expectation is also an attitude. It is a defensive wall we erect in new circumstances to protect the ego from threats to its autonomy within the system.

Notice that in Parmenides, the youth, when in the company of the goddess, exhibits no attitudes whatsoever. He never speaks, even to ask a question. In the presence of divinity, the ego is silent because, being a false entity, it evaporates in the face of an expanded awareness in which it has no legitimate role. In such circumstances, then, we become aware of the illusory nature of the ego, a perception that allows us to recognize its role in the dualities of existence.

All is One, we then realize. Only one world exists, but it has many dimensions and many aspects of being. Parmenides, the Physician of the body, soul and spirit, spoke to several of those seemingly separate systems. In the final fragment of his poem he spoke of the body, but the aim was to integrate body, mind and spirit in unity. In the following fragment, the use of 'forces' points to the causal energies that form the basis of all manifestation.

When male and female mix their seed together in love, the force that shapes the child in the veins, from different blood, can mold a well-proportioned body only if it holds a proper measure. If the forces are in conflict when the seed is joined, and they fail to make a unity, the resulting conflict will plague the growing fetus.

The Greek sense of measure (*metron*) is one of the treasures of ancient culture. A proper sense of measure meant that a person knew who he or she was in the scheme of things. The admonition on the temple walls at Delphi to "Know Thyself" meant to know one's place in the local culture and the cosmos at large, to know what one's proper role was. It did not mean self-knowledge in the existential sense because that would suggest a self-serving, self-concerned attention. We know ourselves when we finally find our true place and calling.

It is a commonplace in these times for many individuals to feel the angst of existential emptiness, to suffer a crisis of meaning. We seek to belong to a community and to feel we have a purpose there, either locally or cosmically. In the absence of that feeling, we work long hours and spend the rest of our time in the techno/pleasure complex of cyberspace or TV-land. In ancient Greece, at the time of Parmenides, the prefix *kyber*, from which we get the term 'cyber' meant 'to steer' and referred to the job of the helmsman. The irony is obvious. Our own cyberspace has an illusory helmsman and is our symbol of psychic loneliness as we wander randomly in cyberspace.

In its best sense, however, what we call cyberspace allows us to participate in a global community of like-minded souls, where connections impossible in earlier times are now made easily. In such a world, physical space and distance has less meaning and fewer limits. Going into inner space, however, has not changed in millennia. It remains as true for us as it did to Parmenides.

The Way of Truth has a clear symbolic focus and direction. To be in harmony with the processes of life, to take part as best we can, and, if we're lucky, to find that still center beyond the world of play, that is what it must be like to stand on the renowned road and hold the right hand of the goddess, who says, "No evil destiny has drawn you here." And in the setting sun, the fire-fangled feathers dangle down.

CHAPTER 5
FROM BEING TO CONSCIOUSNESS

ALTHOUGH THE CONCEPT of Being and its relation to *Nous* and *Logos* was firmly established by Parmenides and, as far as we can trace accurately, was narrowly followed for the next two thousand years through the meandering travels of the Perennial Philosophy, the abandonment of Parmenidean Being as Unity by orthodox thinkers was precipitous, indeed almost immediate. A vestige of the idea was maintained, however, in an isolated concept of *Nous* in Athens, where during the decisive Fifth Century BCE, the abstraction 'Man' and his Mind became the measure (*metron*) of all things (*ta panta*). Leading this shift away from the center of Being and its Royal Road was Anaxagoras – brilliant, engaging, persuasive, and influential – the favorite of Pericles and known among his contemporaries as *Nous*.

It is doubtful, in fact, that the Parthenon would ever have been constructed in all its glory without the influence of Anaxagoras upon Pericles and the Assembly, whose responsibility it was to pay the enormous bills. The new Parthenon, completed in 438 BCE, was a celebration of the new freedom of human consciousness. Sitting poised on the most famous acropolis in the known world, it proclaimed to the intelligentsia a newly achieved freedom from the dominion and destiny of the ancient gods. The Parthenon symbolized for them the exposed forehead of Man, the cerebral cortex loosed from its ancient dreams of the Earth Mother and the wrath of the Sky Father. And Anaxagoras was its earthly creator. Ritually devoted to Athena, the shining edifice was really The Temple of Mind. Just as the mythical Athena had sprung fully grown from the forehead of Zeus, so the Parthenon sprang from acropolis, symbol of the new consciousness in Athens.

All we need do to feel this shift in consciousness is to reflect on fragments 11 and 12 (the Freeman translation) from Anaxagoras' book "On Natural Science," which was on sale for one drachma in Athens at the close of that momentous century. Fragment 11 says, *"In everything there is a portion of everything except Mind; and some things contain Mind also."* The manifest world was a mixture of all things, but Anaxagoras separates out the texture of Mind. He finds that consciousness has a separate identity and nature. Fragment 12 spells it out further.

Other things all contain a part of everything, but Mind is infinite and self-ruling, and is mixed with no Thing, but is alone by itself. If it were not by itself, but were mixed with anything else, it would have had a share of all Things, if it were mixed with anything; for in everything there is a portion of everything, as I said before. And the things mixed (with Mind) would have prevented it, so that it could not rule over any Thing in the same way as it can being alone by itself. For it is the Finest of all Things, and the purest, and has complete understanding of everything, and has the greatest power. All things which have life, both the greater and the less, are ruled by Mind. Mind took command of the universal revolution, so as to make [things] revolve at the outset. And as first things began to revolve from one small point, but now the revolution extends over a greater area, and will spread even further. And the things which were mixed together, and separated off, and divided, were all understood [apprehended] by Mind. And whatever they were going to be, and whatever things were then in existence that are not now, and all things that now exist and whatever shall exist – all were arranged by Mind, as also the revolution now followed by the stars, the sun and moon, and the Air and Aether which were separated off. It was this revolution which caused the separation off. And dense separates from rare, and hot from cold, and bright from dark, and dry from wet. There are many portions of many things. And nothing is absolutely separated off or divided the one from the other except Mind. Mind is all alike, both the greater and the less. But nothing else is like anything else, but each individual thing is and was most obviously that of which it contains the most.

What this vision presents is both startlingly contemporary in both expression and implication and also compelling as formal logic because it emerges from the acquisitive mind of the philosopher as he looks out at the world from the platform of Nous. In other words, the context reflects the order of the observing mind. There is no "mystical transport" here, no "godly" syntax. Alone, Anaxagoras sits on the steps of the Parthenon in Athens and expresses his understanding of how things came to be and how things work. Mind formed the thought, and so Mind must be responsible for all things, or at least for the current condition of all things, because although Mind "arranged" things, it is not clear whether or not Mind initially *created* things. But Anaxagoras seems less interested in the beginning as he is in the process of revolution and Mind's role in managing it all.

We can see in Fragment 12 how easy it would have been in an act of human *hubris* to separate Mind from Being. Indeed,

Fig. 4:
Archaic Kouros
c. 550-500 BCE

Being is not overtly present in the thought of Anaxagoras. The inevitable result of this freeing of Mind as integral to Being marks the growth and eventual dominance of the Sophists in Athens and finally throughout the Hellenic world. Another result of this disconnect was the dramatic change from Archaic to Classical art in the same period. Gone is the ideal form, infused with Being, of the *kouros* and *kore*, with their erect stance and enigmatic smile, right foot forward, with ringlets of hair covering their foreheads; and in their places now stood naturalistic statues of real people, personalities, with high (thinking) foreheads, frowning faces, standing slightly askew, in a disdainful slouch.

Fig. 5:
Late Classical Hermes
c. 420-400 BCE

That slouch would deepen and eventually be absorbed into the superficial decoration that was Roman sculpture.

It is a short step from this change from the integrated vision of Parmenides to the disengagement of the human mind from the divine Mind, which in the Hellenic period becomes totally "other," and most important, not available for communion, except in the mysteries. A crucial separation is implied in the thinking of Anaxagoras, and this separation frames the new age of Hellenic Greece. In its thrall, the famous prophetic sanctuary at Delphi gradually declines in importance as Mind becomes more sovereign in the human being and the divine Mind of Apollo fades and becomes lost in the vague hexameters framed for a price by ambitious temple priests. It is in this environment that the prophetic utterances of the oracle lose credibility. Indeed, the evidence suggests that a growing cynicism gradually envelops Delphi and renders its proclamations meaningless, even ludicrous. By 360 CE Delphi had closed its doors and the waters of speech were no longer bubbling from the sacred spring.[44]

When I said above that the Parmenidean vision of Being was narrowly followed for the next two thousand years, I referred not only to the mysteries but also to the Perennial Philosophy. In the Italian Renaissance it was Marcilio Ficino, under the tutelage of Cosimo De Medici, whose introduction to the *Corpus Hermeticum* contains the following wish for his readers: "that the Divine Mind may glow into your mind and we may contemplate the order of things as they exist in God."[45] Here, Being as Divine Mind is finally restored, still intellectually present and accessible, but it, too, fades from sight in the humanistic claims of the High Renaissance.

We have a glimpse of the movement of Mind in this period in the "Oration on the Dignity of Man" by Ficino's student Pico della Mirandola, who established a new order of freedom for human beings. In this passage, the Master-Builder, or creator god, speaks to Adam:

> *I have placed you at the center of the world . . . Neither heavenly nor earthly, neither mortal nor immortal have We made you and like a judge appointed for being honorable, **you are the molder and maker of yourself; you may sculpt yourself into whatever shape you prefer.** You can grow downward into the lower natures which are brutes or you can again grow upward from the soul's reason into the higher natures which are divine. . . . It is given to man to have that which he chooses and to be that which he wills.*

As stirring as this passage was to the people of the Renaissance from the pen of a young, ecstatic intellect, redolent in its freedom from past constraints, its isolation from participation in Being marks a key separation from any serious notion of unity. By way of a simple, if not simplistic, reductionism, the fall from Being, or what might be called the Vertical Order of the Spirit, to the primacy of the human mind, or what might be termed the Horizontal Order of the World, also finds expression in the works of Machiavelli, whose complete writings characterized the confusion and turbulence of his age. It was as if the famous cave of Plato's Republic became the world writ so large that any earthbound escape was impossible. With no idea or concept of Being present to the human mind, the cave becomes the All, and human destiny must be worked out within its dark confines.

The final separation of mind from Being reaches its formal conclusion in the nineteenth century in light of the philosophy of Hegel. The individual mind becomes the sole source of all knowledge and understanding and is capable, as he argued, of resolving all the problems of philosophy by subsuming mind into a personal system. Being has then left the scene, at least in the philosophical realm, leaving religion to hold up the myths of the past. In Hegel, Mind is self-contained within the individual and, as he put it, we "feel in [our] own self-consciousness all that was previously Beyond."[46]

Even though Hegel's concept of Absolute Mind has religious and spiritual implications, the overall impact of his work and resulting influence on Marxist-Leninism and Existentialism has been a separation of the individual mind from any comprehensive treatment of universal mind, to the point where the human mind is sovereign.

When Mind is severed from Being, the result confines mind (and consciousness) to the human brain and it then must limit itself to looking out, listening, smelling, tasting and feeling the world that confronts it. However, the mind's natural desire to reach out beyond the cave, which lingers from its dim memory of Being, to connect once again to its source, creates the dreaming mind, the imaginative mind, and the creative mind. In turn, these departures from the unified Mind in which we take our life make the metaphors we store in our cultural museums and libraries to remind us that once, long ago, we were part of something larger, more universal. We possessed, in effect, a Parmenidean life.

But now, we can bring Anaxagoras up to date. Back when Anaxagoras spoke of Nous, he was speaking of the active principle of the universe, an organizing force which, as he put it, takes "command of the universal revolution, so as to make (things) revolve at the outset." Contemporary cosmologists don't have trouble with this formulation because "organizing force" does not necessarily imply a conscious force or intelligence. In that formulation, *Nous* can be a description of, or symbol for, the Theory of Everything, or TOE spoken of as the ultimate Unified Field Theory by contemporary physicists. As Stephen Hawking expressed it, if we agree that such an "organizing force" is sufficient, the creator God is no longer necessary. The laws of physics take over for Parmenidean Being, quantum chaos and all.

From Anaxagoras on, then, the gods lose their grip and their authority. They fade into oblivion and, like the Titans of Greek mythology, sleep through eternity in some dark corner of the mythical cosmos. However, the price we pay for this loss is immense, perhaps even fatal, because if the Being of Parmenides dissipates like mist into the vastness of space/time, we *are* truly alone, confined to our little minds, like fireflies blinking on and off in the summer night, oblivious of the winter to come. And worse, any action is deemed possible, resulting in the terrors of the 20th Century, certainly the most brutal, destructive hundred years in human history.

In the face of this loss we can speak now of the need for renewal, to remember once again the sacred reality of our lost heritage, regaining the ground of being as an actual place to stand and as a source of what Voegelin calls "right action." Some prefer, of course, to cling to orthodoxy, secure that buried deep inside the received tradition there dwells personal salvation. Some confine their minds to scientific discovery and the wonders of technology, satisfied with the here and now and the comforts of an illusory progress. But some, a growing number it would appear, are seeking afresh the mysteries of Being in an Eternal Present, hopeful and committed to the active presence of Being as *"the vast unmoving Heart of well-rounded Truth."*

The recovery of Being will not take place solely in the penetrating study and revision of sacred texts, no matter how cleverly we illuminate their hidden meanings and their codified messages. Every seer or prophet who elects to write down his understanding for posterity does so with a certain sadness. A text is useful only as a symbol of the truth, a metaphoric expression of a quest partially undertaken to pass along to succeeding generations. As Emerson put it, books are for idle moments. Our destiny lies in the experience of life, in conscious action. It is no accident that texts flatten "well-rounded truth" into two-dimensional approximations.

Parmenidean Being, on the other hand, expressed as consciousness and the ground of being, is dynamic, unmoving, omnipresent, inclusive, and absolute. Only through the mindful attention to experience we will find that we can grasp what is dynamic and comprehend what is unmoving and come to know for ourselves the nature of what is omnipresent, inclusive and absolute. The experience necessary to such understanding comes through the full range of human expression: the physical, emotional, intellectual and spiritual nature of human being.

If we look at the five attributes of Being and the four aspects of human nature, we can discover just how the quest for the ground is to be undertaken and what the interface with Being might resemble. Nothing partial will suffice. Human consciousness, if it desires to participate with Being, will emanate from all four human faculties functioning as a whole. The quest, in other words, is simultaneously physical, emotional, intellectual and spiritual. The interface (Plato's *metaxy*) will always embody the five attributes of Being. Therefore, our experience of Being will be felt fully and have the dynamic effects of transparency (a seeing through surfaces), of omnipresence (Being as everywhere), of inclusion (not feeling separate from anyone or anything) and absolute (a perception of there not being anything greater or fuller).

Human Genius As The Path To Being

Pico della Mirandola's declaration of freedom following from a separation from Being results in a paradox that well may signal a potential for the recovery of Being in a transformational leap of being. The powerful impulse to recover the ground finds its human expression in genius – in physical, emotional, intellectual and spiritual symbols of the attributes of Being.

The Great Leap of Being recognized by Voegelin and others from 500 BC texts was the result of the death of the mythological vision of the gods. Human genius rose into the silence from Olympus and Sinai to remake the human/divine relationship. Great teachers arose, great art flourished, and a Golden Age of human consciousness flooded the Mediterranean basin all the way to the Indus River.

Again in 1450 CE Florence, a flowering filled the vacuum created by political and religious chaos to gradually fill Europe with works of genius and a new enlightenment which lasted into the Romantic Idealism of the nineteenth century, only to be overcome by the Industrial Revolution and the triumph of materialism. But in the Renaissance the genius of Marcilio Ficino, Pico, Fra Angelico, Giotto, Leonardo and Michaelangelo filled a void as eruptions of consciousness reached into the expanding universe discovered a century later by Galileo.

But this is not meant to be a history. The present transformation is taking place in a global context of participation and creativity. On the physical level, in sport, for example, human beings are flexing their muscles in extraordinary ways, showing the power, grace, rhythm, speed, and flexibility of the human body.

These qualities mirror at the level of body the attributes of Being, and the feeling of awe in the presence of such performance, be it athlete, acrobat, or dancer, resembles the awe of the youth in the presence of the goddess.

So too in matters of the intellect, whether it be the wonders of scientific genius of the New Physics in unraveling the mysteries of the cosmos or the technical skill in developing a quantum computer capable of crunching numbers at prodigious rates. Such expansion and inventiveness of mind is also a reflection and embodiment of the attributes of Being. And as long as we as human beings remember that in the glow of new light that the dark corners of mystery remain to be penetrated as well as celebrated, we will avoid the kind of messiah complexes that plague those who are convinced of their "special" destiny and end by destroying themselves and their deluded followers.

The correct perspective and balance has always, at least for Americans, been Emerson's. He spoke accurately in "Nominalist and Realist" on the matter of truth, when he said, "I cannot often enough say, that a man is only a relative and representative nature. Each is a hint of the truth, but far enough from being that truth, which yet he quite newly and inevitably suggests to us." It is clear in remarks such as these that Emerson maintained a self-effacing humility throughout his revelatory career, which kept him free of idolatry by the masses. And yet, his mind was free of the materialist reductionism that followed Romanticism and was also free of the theological orthodoxy that confined his contemporaries.

Emerson avoided the trap of assigning attributes to his Oversoul, referring to it only as the Universal Mind accessible to human perception and understanding, but refraining from providing it with tangible symbols. And that's as it should be. If he had intimated that Universal Mind was "the organizing principle" of creation, that phrase would have been seized upon by the orthodox as proof of Emerson's apostasy.

But if Emerson in his own time appeared to vacillate between Unitarian tradition and deist pantheism, we in ours cannot do the same. If we desire seriously to re-vision Being without the "sacred transport" of Parmenides, the infinite Mind of Anaxagoras, or the Oversoul of Emerson, we have to assign symbols that are vibrant with dynamic possibility, alive with potential, and infinite in scope. And, in our own time and way of approaching reality, I would also say we cannot lapse into hierarchies, as Plotinus did and as other Neoplatonists were and are wont to do. Neither vertical nor horizontal imagery will suffice. Being is integral, infusing its essence into every particle of matter and energy, as thoroughly organic and dynamic as it is subtle and infinite.

If, as Heraclitus said, "all things are One," then Being is that aspect of the One in which we take our life and within which the cosmos is animated. The symbol that most approximates that inclusive condition is a matrix of pervasive conscious energy, which, as we currently understand it, animates all things. Being is, arguably, intelligent or coherent energy, infinite in potential, scope and also coherent in content. It is this last assertion that troubles physicists, who cannot find the experimental framework to test such a hypothesis. Most would accept energy, replacing Classic formulations of matter, as the all-embracing character of everything that is, the Greek *ta panta*. Whether or not that energy is conscious or not is the subject of current debate in the theoretical physics community, and it may be possible to see empirical proof of a universal consciousness emerging from theoretical physics rather than philosophy.

As practiced in the academy, philosophy will not be the means by which Being is re-imagined and made manifest. As Voegelin observed in *Anamnesis*, "Eternal being did not wait for philosophy in order to realize itself in time."[47] The tools for such analysis will include theoretical physics, mathematics (the dynamics of number), geometry, art and language. In all these cases, or disciplines, the mode of investigation is symbolic representation, this in contrast to similar kinds of investigation undertaken by the traditional sciences.

For example, the relatively new field of Consciousness Studies is currently the means by which mind as an entity is being investigated. Most of the work, however, is now being done in neurobiology, neuro-pharmachology, and chemistry, using technical language and traditional investigative methods in a narrow range of research. The results will be expressed as the data of experimentation and will of necessity be limited to that data. If Being is dynamic, unmoving, omnipresent, inclusive, and absolute, then its symbolic representations must express those attributes a well. It will take an Einstein of the mind to effect a breakthrough.

Short of that outcome, we can begin a recovery of Being with a brief passage from Voegelin's *Anamnesis* in a chapter entitled "The Consciousness of the Ground."

The intentional character of participating consciousness becomes a central theme in the generation of philosophers about 500 B.C. Parmenides says it is the same thing to think (*noein*) and to be (*einai*); and Heraclitus uses the term *logos* in a double meaning of exegetic thinking and explained reality. A *trias* [triad] of being-thinking-symbol is a reality identical with itself and, at the same time, analytically kept distinct as being. Noetic consciousness is the luminosity in which thinking about reality finds its language, and in this linguistic expression it again relates itself to reality.[48]

It is the sentence "A *trias* of being-thinking-symbol is a reality identical with itself and, at the same time, analytically kept distinct as being" that challenges us.[49] Voegelin wishes to demonstrate that thinking by itself yields only thought about thought, folding in on itself in existential self-consciousness, leading nowhere. Being, by itself, is necessarily beyond human investigation by traditional means. Symbol, by itself, is disconnected, localized in meaning. Therefore, the desired condition is a dynamic triad of being-thinking-symbol that is "identical with itself" in a dynamic relation of interacting forces, capable of participation. Within the individual, this triad is best described as a potential state consisting of consciousness, being, and symbolic representation (or thingness).

The symbol 'ground' in relation to being is the necessary third point which creates stability within the dual (thus unstable) tension of thinking-being. A consciousness of the ground of being is a noetic experience crucial to the understanding. Individuals fortunate enough to have this experience of the ground become aware of the structure of consciousness within themselves in relation to that ground and are able to express that awareness in language symbols, which throughout history have come down to us as myth, poetry, philosophy and textual exegesis.

How these individuals experience the ground depends on how the four human attributes are arranged. In some, the experience will be physical, expressed by harmonies of movement leading to a fusion with surrounding reality with or without other human beings; or it may be emotional, expressed by heightened feelings of unity with being, an overwhelming outpouring of love and compassion or awareness of inner warmth; or intellectual, expressed by flashes of insight or visions of the Infinite; or, in rarer circumstances, it may be spiritual, expressed by mystical visions or the experience of unity.

In any of these cases, the faculty of discrimination will be an essential ingredient in the quest. The insight into Voegelin's triad of being-thinking-symbol will never be expressed as a system, which by definition is a closed structure attracting adherents. The ground, in other words, will not appear as the symbol "religion" or "scientific theory" or "person." By definition, these symbols cannot express the attributes of Being. Even the word 'ground' carries with it connotations of earth, foundation, or fixed place.

It should be clear that terms-as-symbols such as "Christianity," "Islam," "Jesus Christ," or "Buddha," to name a few, do not meet the criteria for Being, or for that matter even the triad of being-thinking-symbol formulated by Voegelin. If unity is to be a test, then only the trinity-as-one as a dynamic expression of relations will suffice.

The result of this formulation is that personal participation at the noetic level is a requirement for the existence of being perceived as the ground. A further requirement involves an acceptance of such existence as both meaningful and positive. The presence of despair or revolt in consciousness renders human life intolerable and makes impossible the connection to Being. The body of work left by French Existentialism in the 1940s and 50s illustrates the point.

The key to the noetic quest for the ground of being depends first on the divesting of what Voegelin refers to as "ersatz realities."[50] Typical of these are formulations such as philosophical systems, political ideologies, and all manner of isms, including postmodernism, collectivism, scientism, and so on. These stances in the world make the "thinking" part of the triad much more difficult. When the goddess instructs the youth in Parmenides' poem, she tells him that it is important to learn the opinions of men so that he can guard against false notions, or "ersatz realities." As the psychologists tell us, we are programmed in these isms from an early age, often fitting ourselves into one or more of them for a lifetime.

Once we rid ourselves of these illusions, what remains? Are we meant to systematically empty our memory of all such programs? And what would such de-programming involve? Rather than entering some sort of ideological rehabilitation program, the more positive approach is to engage the faculty of observation. The desired state is a reflective waiting upon the presence of Being in order to know its structure and laws. Such waiting can of course be a life-long quest with no dramatic moment of insight or realization. Or there can grow within a quiet confidence in the reality of the ground and its intimacy. In the meantime, however, the thoughtful mind can practice the necessary discipline by attending to the hidden laws of nature, because nature, including the human instrument, is a symbol of being and contains within its structures all the data we require.

Returning once more to the attributes of Being, it is useful to remember that Being does not "exist" in the sense we human beings experience that word. We experience thought and different levels of consciousness, but seldom the existence of Being except through rare moments of insight. And even then, we experience Being through certain attributes, like the quality of inclusion, for example, or through love and tolerance, which can be experienced physically, emotionally, intellectually and spiritually in our relations and contacts with others. So, too, with the other attributes of Being. In other words, we can know the nature of Being through its attributes in the world of experience.

In sum, human beings possess the capacity for knowing Being as the result of participation in existence. Desire and knowing together become luminous as consciousness. The Greek *Nous* is the organ of being, not a separate an isolated human faculty. It manifests in the human being as the organ of knowing, and its *logos* is its order in the world. Consciousness is relational, connecting all things, including ourselves, to Being. All things are full of Being. Human being is a tensional existence between states of consciousness, much of the time asleep, rarely awake, with some yearning to know Being.

Human beings learn to experience the world as duality, a necessary tension that is formally incorporated into systems of learning about the way the world works. We literally forget, immersed as we are in experience, that all is one, with the result that we feel separate and isolated from one another, except that also we sometimes remember and in that remembering we experience love. Love is the form of Being. Love redeems us from duality.

In the time of Parmenides, the dying world of myth encountered the new world of philosophy, and in the resulting tension, consciousness evolved to a different understanding of Being. A new spirit emerged, essentially male in character, and it swept away the ancient matriarchal world of myth-o-poetic order.

Presently, we await another impulse, the character of which no one can predict, although, following Jungian thought, it may emerge as a feminine impulse. Indications of its coming are everywhere. We know only that its scope will be planetary and that, once again, consciousness will evolve as its sign. Its appearance will possess the attributes of being: dynamic, unmoving, omnipresent, inclusive, and absolute, but be expressed in human terms through genius and its capacity for love. tolerance, harmony, and peace.

Glossary

The following Greek terms are central to an understanding of Parmenides. The English equivalents will vary in other contexts.

aletheia – objective truth, an uncovering what has been forgotten

ananke – necessity

atremes – immovable

Dike – Justice

doxa – human opinion (false views)

eon – Being

eros – Love, also the Spirit, born of Plenty and Poverty

eukyklos – well-rounded, spherical

hodos – path or road

logos – logical argument, domain of the Word, realm of being

metaxy – in-between, the interface of human and divine correspondence

nous – mind, an organ of the human soul which grasps Being
also, an organ of Being, later, the intellect

Suggested Reading

Those interested in exploring Parmenides further might find the following books useful.

Cordero, Nestor-Luis. *By Being, It Is* (Parmenides Publishing) 2004

Curd, Patricia. The Legacy of Parmenides, (Parmenides Publishing) 2004

Geldard, Richard. *Remembering Heraclitus* (Lindisfarne Books) 2000

Heideger, Martin. *Parmenides* (Indiana University Press) 1992

Kingsley, Peter. *In the Dark Places of Wisdom* (Golden Sufi Center) 1999

Kirk, G. S. Raven, J.E., Schofield, M. *The Presocratic Philosophers* (Cambridge university Press, Cambridge, 2nd edition, 1983

ENDNOTES

1. Richard Geldard, *Heraclitus Remembered*, Lindisfarne, 2000.

2. Katherine Freeman, *Ancilla To The Presocratic Philosophers*, Harvard University Press, Cambridge, 1948).

3. Ibid.

4. Francis Cornford, *Plato and Parmenides*, Liberal Arts Press, New York, 1957, p.3

5. Giorgio de Santillana, *Reflections on Men and Ideas*, M.I.T. Press, Cambridge, 1968, p103

6. "On Nature" (*peri physis*) was written in broken dactylic hexameters. The dactylic foot – a strong beat followed by two short beats – does not translate well into English, where the iambic foot – short, long – is more natural.

7. Fragment numbering follows Freeman.

8. *The Bhagavad Gita*, trans. Shri Purohit Swami, Faber and Faber, London, 1978, p. 83

9. Giorgio de Santillana, *Reflections on Men and Ideas*, M.I.T. Press, Cambridge, 1968, p. 94.

10. It is worth pointing out that the zodiac does not divide conveniently into neat 30-degree arcs through the 360 degrees of the Precession. Some constellations are larger than others. As a result, there is some discrepancy as to when, exactly, the Age of Aquarius should begin.

11. *Hermetica*, vol. 1, edited and translated by Walter Scott, Shambhala, Boston, 1985, p. 115

12. Hesiod, Theogeny, Works and Days, trans. A. Athanassakis, Johns Hopkins University Press, Baltimore and London, 1983, p. 13

13. Some modern commentators have even suggested that the grammatical difficulties arise from the awkwardness of Parmenides as a poet, that he couldn't express the idea more clearly. This sort of argument arises from the arrogance of modern scholars looking back condescendingly at the primitive peoples of the past.

14. The Uncertainty Principle of quantum mechanics tells us that nothingness is not possible. In fact, nothingness is explicitly forbidden. "Quantum Theory Tugged, And All of Physics Unraveled," New York Times, December 12, 2000.

15. Plato, *The Republic*, Book VII, 532c

16. Plato, *Collected Dialogues*, ed. Hamilton and Cairns, Princeton University Press, 1961, p. 920

17. Ibid, p. 922

18. Ibid, p. 1589

19. Ibid, "Philebus," p. 1092 (16c-d)

20. Ibid, p. 1093 (17e)

21. Astrid Fitzgerald, "Harmony by Design," *Parabola Magazine, The Golden Mean*, Winter 1991, Vol. XVI, N¼¼ 4, ISSN: 0362-1596).

22. These three forces correspond to the Hindu forces of Rajas, Tamas and Sattva, which rule the universe as well as human nature.

23. Aristotle, "Mataphysics," Book I, Part 3

24. Ibid

25. Ibid, Part 5

26. Friedrich Schelling, "The Deities of Samothrace," AAR Studies in Religion, ed. Robert F. Brown, Scholar's Press, Missoula, Montana, 1977, p. 18

27. Friedrich Schelling, *First Outline of a System of the Philosophy of Nature*, SUNY Press, Albany, 2004.

28. Eric Voegelin, "Israel and Revelation," Louisiana State University Press, Baton Rouge and London, 1956, p. 376.

29. Eric Voegelin, "The Eclipse of Reality," Collected Works, vol. 28, Louisiana State University Press, Baton Rouge, 1990, p. 156

30. Eric Voegelin, "On Schelling's Promethean Grace," *Collected Works*, vol. 25, p. 220.

31. Eric Voegelin, *The World of the Polis*, Louisiana State University Press, Baton Rouge and London, 1957, p. 203. Hereafter cited as Polis

32. *Polis*, p. 206.

33. *Polis*, p. 207.

34. *Polis*, p. 208.

35. *Polis*, p. 209.

36. Eric Voegelin, *In Search of Order*, Louisiana State University Press, Baton Rouge and London, 1987, p. 88. Hereafter cited as Search

37. *Search*, p. 89.

38. *Polis*, p. 208-209.

39. Sri Aurobindo, *The Supermental Manifestation*, Sri Aurobindo Ashram, Pondicherry, 1997, p. 129.

40. Ibid, p. 383.

41. Eric Voegelin, *The Ecumenic Age*, Louisiana State University Press, Baton Rouge and London, 1974, p. 186.

42. "Symposioum," 211, e

43. Ibid, 212, a

44. See *The Oracle* (Penguin, 2006) by William Broad for the latest research on the origins and authenticity of the oracle at Delphi.

45. Eric Voegelin, *In Search of Order*, p. 63

46. Ibid, p. 62.

47. Eric Voegelin, *Anamnesis*, University of Missouri Press, 1978, p. 116

48. Ibid, p. 167.

49. Voegelin appears to be using the Greek trias in the Pythagorean sense of a dynamic set of three.

50. Ibid, p. 172.

Printed in the USA
CPSIA information can be obtained
at www.ICGtesting.com
JSHW082213140824
68134JS00014B/595